Multiple Intelligences and Instructional Technology

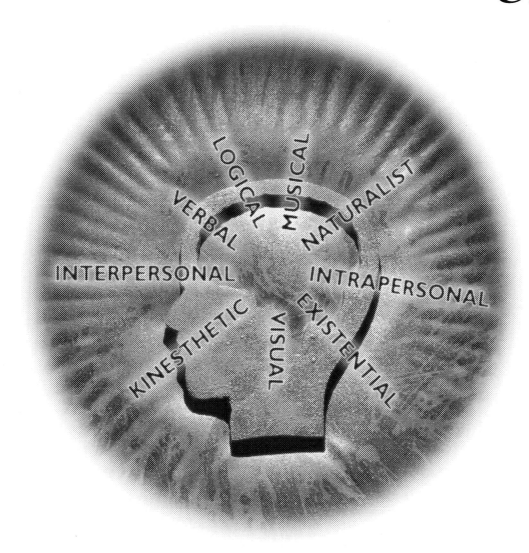

A Manual for Every Mind

Walter McKenzie

Multiple Intelligences and Instructional Technology
A Manual for Every Mind

Walter McKenzie

DIRECTOR OF PUBLISHING
Jean Marie Hall

ACQUISITIONS EDITOR
Mathew Manweller

BOOK PUBLISHING PROJECT MANAGER
Tracy Cozzens

DATA AND COMMUNICATIONS MANAGER
Diannah Anavir

ADMINISTRATIVE ASSISTANT
Pam Calegari

COPY EDITOR
Ron Renchler, The Electronic Page

COVER DESIGN
Katherine Getta, Getta Graphic Design

BOOK DESIGN
Katherine Getta, Getta Graphic Design

LAYOUT AND PRODUCTION
Tracy Cozzens

International Society for Technology in Education (ISTE)
480 Charnelton Street
Eugene, OR 97401-2626
Order Desk: 1.800.336.5191
Order Fax: 1.541.302.3778
Customer Service: orders@iste.org
Books and Courseware: books@iste.org
Permissions: permissions@iste.org
World Wide Web: www.iste.org

First Edition
ISBN 1-56484-192-8

About ISTE

The International Society for Technology in Education (ISTE) is a nonprofit professional organization with a worldwide membership of leaders in educational technology. We are dedicated to promoting appropriate uses of information technology to support and improve learning, teaching, and administration in K–12 education and teacher education. As part of that mission, ISTE provides high-quality and timely information, services, and materials, such as this book.

The ISTE Publishing Department works with experienced educators to develop and produce classroom-tested books and courseware. We look for content that emphasizes the use of technology where it can make a difference—making the teacher's job easier; saving time; motivating students; helping students who have unique learning styles, abilities, or backgrounds; and creating learning environments that would be impossible without technology. We believe technology can improve the effectiveness of teaching while making learning exciting and fun.

Every manuscript and product we select for publication is peer reviewed and professionally edited. While we take pride in our publications, we also recognize the difficulties of maintaining quality while keeping on top of the latest technologies and research. Please let us know what products you would find helpful. We value your feedback on this book and other ISTE products. E-mail us at **books@iste.org**.

ISTE is home of the National Educational Technology Standards (NETS) Project and the National Center for Preparing Tomorrow's Teachers to Use Technology (NCPT3). To learn more about NETS or request a print catalog, visit our Web site at **www.iste.org**, which provides:

- Current educational technology standards for K–12 student and teacher education
- A bookstore with online ordering and membership discount options
- *Learning & Leading with Technology* magazine
- *ISTE Update*, membership newsletter
- Teacher resources
- Discussion groups
- Professional development services, including national conference information
- Research projects
- Member services

About the Author

Walter McKenzie is a teacher, trainer, and consultant who has been incorporating technology and multiple intelligences theory into instruction over the past decade. He serves as chair for the Department of Instruction at Connected University, where he has authored and taught a class on teaching multiple intelligences through technology. He is an instructional technology coordinator for the Arlington, Virginia, Public Schools and has presented on multiple intelligences, technology integration, and creative education around the country. He hosts the One and Only Surfaquarium, an education Web site (http://surfaquarium.com); and his weekly newsletter *Innovative Teaching* currently boasts more than 2,800 subscribers. He resides in Virginia with his wife Carleen and his children Christopher and Mallory.

Dedication

This book is dedicated to educators everywhere who are rising to meet the challenge of education in the Information Age. Special thanks to Sheryl Asen for her guidance as friend and editor, and to my family for lending me the time and support to make this book a reality.

Contents

Figures and Tables

Figures

Tables

Preface

I want to share with you the possibilities for Dr. Howard Gardner's multiple intelligences (MI) theory as it relates to technology and instruction. These intelligences are each viable, distinct pathways to learning; they are ways of knowing that stand on their own two feet and yet act in consort with even greater power. They are not talents, gifts, aptitudes, or learning styles. The words "talents," "gifts," and "aptitudes" each connotes an ability above and beyond the realm of simple human understanding, such as the ability to play a musical instrument well or set new records in athletic competitions. Learning styles are fixed modes of understanding that a learner uses regardless of the instructional context. Intelligences are more than either of these. They are legitimate conduits of cognition that can be flexibly applied by all learners across the curriculum in varied contexts.

Although we each have all the intelligences, they are distributed uniquely in each of us. Because of this there is a tendency to want to label learners by specific intelligences. Gardner is adamantly opposed to this. He sees his theory as a way to empower learners, not to diagnose deficits and prescribe remediation. Therefore, I avoid discussing "types" of learners and the suggestion that there are surefire types of instruction and technology that accommodate specific learner strengths. Analyzing instruction by intelligences is one thing, but once it is done we need to rebuild that instruction so that it is once again holistic when delivered in the classroom.

Through my presentations on MI theory around the country, I have met teachers who are full of excitement and questions as we consider the implications of Gardner's work. Many teachers indicate that they are already very familiar with his theory and that they are ready to learn ways to implement his work systematically in the classroom. I am always delighted to work with these dedicated people to help them explore the possibilities for instruction. I am often asked if there is one quick and easy way to accommodate the intelligences in the classroom. Indeed, there are books on the market today that try to capitalize on this desire for one neatly packaged, surefire way to realize the promise of MI. Those who truly know Gardner's work, though, understand that to realize its full potential we have to dig deeper.

In writing this book I want to address this need teachers express for concrete approaches to using MI and technology in the classroom. There is a huge void between Gardner's vision and its successful implementation in instruction. There is no prepackaged MI program that will faithfully follow MI theory, just as there is no psychometric instrument that will accurately measure these varied kinds of intelligences. Yes, there are people out there willing to sell such promises and products to you if you have the money, but stand firm by your convictions and don't be a soft sell!

It is my hope that this book will provide the structure you need to successfully begin implementing Gardner's work in your classroom. You will discover all sorts of possibilities for bringing in technology and other materials to augment your instruction, and they will be your choices because you know what is most appropriate and effective in your classroom. It is my hope that you will be empowered by the possibilities you discover!

Walter McKenzie

Chapter 1

A New Theory of Learning

Ever since I was first introduced to Howard Gardner's theory of multiple intelligences (MI), my views of intelligence and instruction have changed. Where I once was trained to see learning deficits, I now recognized untapped potential. Old instructional practices started to give way to new approaches to teaching and learning. It became clear to me over time that, while Gardner was proposing a theory of intelligence, its application for the classroom was as a learning theory. There are now new paths to learning, paths that have gone long unexplored. Along the way, many students have been left taking only the traditional pathway of education.

A Letter from Paul

Consider a letter I received from Paul a couple of years ago. It touched me in a profound way, not unlike Gardner's work itself.

Dear Walter,

I am very glad I found your Web page (http://surfaquarium.com/im.htm). We all would like to think we are smart. Could you help me with three problems I have? One, I think ALL the time, but noise like TV and radio distract me. Two, I can look at anything and see it in three dimensions. And three, I always am looking on things that relate in forms and genealogies. I want to believe I have some smarts. I am a dreamer, a visionary, a futurist, yet cannot use those talents to their fullest ability. I am 56 years old and retired. Do you think I am different than the "normal" crowd, and why? Your answer is very important to me. Even if your answer is negative it cannot hurt my feelings.

Paul

After some consideration of this heartfelt inquiry, I provided Paul with the following response:

Dear Paul,

Thanks for writing. Gardner stresses how culturally based intelligence is. What constitutes genius in the U.S. today is totally useless in Micronesia. The kinds of intelligence you describe to me are visual, naturalist, and logical. Visual and naturalist intelligences have not traditionally been valued in our society, and at 56 you probably had a hard row to hoe trying to find your niche in the middle of this century in our culture. It amazes me how much suffering people have had to endure because their mental strengths were not the ones schools or businesses emphasized. I can tell from the tone of your letter that you have felt troubled because of this tendency in our society.

The good news is that society is going through great change. Whereas visual thinkers used to be classified as artists and architects, and naturalists used to be labeled as environmentalists and academics, now someone of your abilities has options to realize his or her potential as a visionary—an idea person who thinks "outside the box." In my experience, visual thinkers are some of the most creative because they look at ideas in nontraditional, nonverbal ways. Likewise, naturalists are creative in that they organize and analyze things in ways that are different from the traditional linear, logical approach. In short, Paul, you are still young and so many things are getting more emphasis in our culture that lots of doors are opening up for you. Companies are looking for people with nonconventional ideas and new ways to solve their very old problems.

The biggest thing you'll want to work on is shedding the years of frustration and disappointment that you have endured because you didn't fit the traditional mode of intelligence espoused 50 years ago. That leaves a lot of scars, but you can get past them if you allow yourself the opportunity to start over and see yourself as the truly gifted person you are. Dr. Gardner would be standing here telling you the exact same thing. Society has used models of intelligence to label and limit individuals for too long. Gardner's model is meant to empower all people, to let all of us shine and realize our full potential. I invite you to read some of his work and come to understand everything you have to offer the rest of us.

Hope this helps!

Walter

There is still time for Paul to realize his potential and know what it is like to use his talents because those old Industrial Age assumptions are changing quickly in society. I often think of Paul and wonder how he is doing these days. For him, MI theory means more than Gardner may have ever realized.

Here is Paul's response to my original letter:

Dear Walter,

Thank you for your quick response to my inquiry. Thank you for the encouragement and information you have given me. I have no love for the educational system in my time growing up. It is my hope with this newfound gift I can help others find their potential also. Your response has given me hope and glimmer of what I can become if I apply myself with these gifts.

Paul

For Paul the hope of new possibilities shines in his reply. Isn't it amazing how the weight of the years is lifted from his shoulders as he realizes what the future might hold for him? Paul is highly aware of his abilities; he just needed to know that he could meaningfully use them to contribute to society. The messages he received as a student did not validate his strengths. In fact, his sense of purpose and worth were undermined as he struggled to fit into the prevailing definition of what was valued as intelligence.

Along came Howard Gardner, who challenged the prevailing definition of intelligence with one concise description of what it means to be smart: "the ability to find and solve problems and create products of value in one's own culture." It's so simple it's profound! There is no single measurement for intelligence in this definition. There is no "quotient" that can quantify ability or predict potential.

Gardner's theory attempts to provide for the complex processes of human cognition without setting limits on its potential. If the human mind has an operating system, Gardner's model is the manual that attempts to explain how it runs.

21st-Century Skills

The metaphor of an operating system has become commonplace with the explosion of information technology over the past several decades. Students today are facing a job market built around an emerging information economy, and the "three Rs" will not sufficiently prepare students for the 21st-century workplace. While reading, writing, mathematics, and citizenship are still core components of American education, the Information Age demands that people need additional skills to remain competitive. Workers need the following skills:

- **INFORMATION TECHNOLOGY SKILLS**—the ability to access information and manipulate it using a variety of digital tools.

- **INFORMATION LITERACY SKILLS**—the ability to evaluate information for validity and reliability through a variety of critical-thinking strategies.

- **PROBLEM-SOLVING SKILLS**—the ability to generate efficient, effective solutions that meet the needs of the marketplace.

- **COLLABORATION SKILLS**—the ability to interact with colleagues, even in geographically disparate locations, to complete complex tasks.

- **FLEXIBILITY**—the ability to adapt and adjust ideas as new information becomes available.

- **CREATIVITY**—the ability to present information and ideas in novel or unique ways in the marketplace.

Individually, each of these skills is already valued in the workplace. In combination, however, they create a profile of a worker functioning in a much more abstract environment in which goals and expectations change quickly. As we become the world's information superpower, the emphasis will be more on teamwork and the marketing of ideas than on concrete products.

The Information Age

With the Information Age evolving so rapidly, how do schools adopt a new model of thinking and learning that adequately parallels society's demands? The change is already taking place in classrooms across the country. But if as teachers we tend to teach in the same ways that we ourselves were taught, how then do we break away from the standardized, homogeneous approach to schooling that we knew as students? On what sound theory can those innovators in the classroom who have already recognized the changing needs of society base their evolving instructional practices?

Gardner's MI theory does an excellent job of addressing the needs of the Information Age. In fact, his intelligences nicely correspond to the very skills we have just discussed:

- **INFORMATION TECHNOLOGY SKILLS**—the kinesthetic intelligence supports these skills as students manipulate tools that help them to work successfully with information.

- **INFORMATION LITERACY SKILLS**—the intrapersonal and naturalist intelligences come into play as students identify and evaluate information for its usefulness.

- **PROBLEM-SOLVING SKILLS**—the logical intelligence operates as students offer varied ideas to solve problems.

- **COLLABORATION SKILLS**—the interpersonal and linguistic intelligences function when students interact to complete tasks and create products for the greater good.

- **FLEXIBILITY**—the musical intelligence allows students to detect and follow patterns in information as it becomes available.

- **CREATIVITY**—the visual and existential intelligences allow students to envision ideas, solutions, and products that can improve the quality of their lives.

Perhaps there has never been a better time for Gardner's ideas to take hold. They seem to answer so many questions and address so many needs in society. Perhaps this is why educators at so many levels have embraced it so readily.

As the old saying goes, "If the only tool you have is a hammer, everything around you looks like a nail." The tools of technology provide us with a rare opportunity to redefine how and what we teach. There is no longer a one-size-fits-all solution for providing instruction. This is a time of great growth that can also be a time of great peril. Because technology advances so quickly it's very easy to be impressed by new advancements, even to the point of letting the technology supercede the kinds and quality of instruction we provide. As educators we have a responsibility to make sure that these tools are well grounded in sound theory and practice. If instructional technology isn't built on a sound instructional foundation, it won't fulfill its promise. It will fall by the wayside like many other innovations that have preceded it. Gardner's theory offers that strong theoretical foundation for the integration of technology into education.

Resources Accompanying This Book

This book is meant to be a practical guide for applying Gardner's MI theory to education by integrating instructional technology into the curriculum. To make the book as useful as possible, a variety of resources and tools have been included both in the book itself and on the accompanying CD-ROM.

Among these resources are two MI surveys: one text-based survey for older students (see Appendix A) and one image-based survey for students in primary grades (see Appendix B).

The Primary Grades Multiple Intelligences Survey, which is a series of pictures highlighting specific activities, comes in two formats. The student version has no captions under the pictures. The Teacher Scoring Key (on the CD-ROM) includes captions identifying the intelligence being indicated, allowing for easy interpretation of student responses.

The Multiple Intelligence Survey for Students, which is for older students, also comes in two versions. The black and white version is for students, and the color-coded version is for teachers who wish to analyze survey items or break down student responses by intelligence. Both versions are Microsoft Excel format for easy calculation and analysis by intelligence. Chapter 2 explains the use of the surveys in more detail. Both surveys and both teacher scoring keys appear on the CD-ROM.

Also included in the book and on the CD-ROM are lesson, unit, and collaborative unit templates for constructing MI-based instruction. A software evaluation tool and PEP, POMAT, and OPP charts for analyzing existing lessons and resources are also provided.

It is my hope that these tools will assist you in successfully transforming your classroom into a technology-rich, intelligence-wise learning environment.

Reflections

1 What is the difference between viewing MI as a theory of intelligence and a theory of learning?

2 How does today's classroom differ from the classroom of the Industrial Age?

3 In what ways do you teach the way you were taught? In what ways do you teach the way children learn?

Chapter 2

Instructional Design and Multiple Intelligences

Since Howard Gardner first introduced his multiple intelligences (MI) theory, educators have been grappling with its implications. Gardner himself does not presume to superimpose his model on teaching and learning but rather defers to educators as the experts who can best apply his work in the classroom. To make this happen, teachers first need to know the distinguishing characteristics of each of the intelligences. This is important because in many cases we take an intelligence at face value without truly examining it for its distinct attributes and features. Too often, for example, teachers assume that musical intelligence is merely the introduction of music into a lesson, or that the naturalist intelligence is simply the study of flora and fauna in the curriculum. If we are going to effectively transform instruction by using Gardner's theory, we must understand it in its basic tenets. To do any less would be to not give it its due as a viable model.

Intelligences Overview

Let's take a brief look at each intelligence before discussing technology.

> **VERBAL/LINGUISTIC**—Traditionally one of the heavily emphasized intelligences in the classroom. It has been valued because it matches the way we traditionally have taught: lecture, recitation, textbooks, and board work. It includes the ability to express oneself orally and in writing, as well as the ability to master foreign languages.

> **LOGICAL/MATHEMATICAL**—Also highly valued in traditional instruction. It is not simply the intelligence of mathematics but of logic and reasoning. This intelligence allows us to be problem solvers. It seeks structure in the learning environment and thrives on sequenced, orderly lessons. In the traditional classroom, students are asked to conform to the teacher's instructional approach, and this intelligence allows them to do so.

> **VISUAL/SPATIAL**—Provides for spatial reasoning through the use of charts, graphs, maps, tables, illustrations, art, puzzles, costumes, and many other materials. As educators, we are instinctively aware of this intelligence. The visual/spatial intelligence allows students to picture ideas and solutions to problems in their minds before they are able to verbalize them or put them into practice.

> **BODILY/KINESTHETIC**—The intelligence of active learning. The kinesthetic intelligence is promoted through fine and gross motor activities, such as manipulative learning centers, science labs, active games, and dramatic improvisations. Students with a strong bodily/kinesthetic intelligence may tend to

seem overactive in the traditional classroom, but they thrive in hands-on learning environments.

MUSICAL/RHYTHMIC—The intelligence of patterns, including songs, poetry, instruments, environmental sounds, and response to rhythms. By picking up the patterns in different situations, learners are able to make sense of their environment and adapt successfully. Note that this is not exclusively an auditory intelligence; it can include all kinds of patterns.

INTRAPERSONAL—The intelligence of feelings, values, and attitudes. The intrapersonal intelligence helps the learner make an affective connection with the curriculum. Children who ask, "Why do I need to learn this?" or "Is this policy fair?" are exercising their intrapersonal intelligence. It is the part of us that expects learning to be meaningful.

INTERPERSONAL—The intelligence that provides for social learning in all its forms. Interpersonal intelligence requires social interaction in order to make sense of learning. Students with a strong interpersonal tendency may have been labeled "too talkative" in the traditional classroom. They thrive in cooperative groups where they work with partners, and even in whole-group instruction where they are free to ask, discuss, and understand.

NATURALIST—The intelligence of categories and hierarchies. While the naturalist intelligence does include the study of plants, animals, and other sciences, consider the processes that these disciplines promote: classification, categorization, and hierarchical frameworks. Biologists, botanists, zoologists, archaeologists, and geologists have been classifying and categorizing for centuries by using their naturalist intelligence.

EXISTENTIAL—The human response to being alive in all ways. It can include aesthetics, philosophy, and religion and emphasizes the classical values of beauty, truth, and goodness. The existential intelligence allows students to see their place in the big picture, be it in the classroom, community, world, or universe. Gardner is still not satisfied that he has enough physiologic brain evidence to conclusively establish this as an intelligence, but he has been considering establishing it the ninth intelligence. I am including it here for the purposes of our discussion. After all, who has not observed this intelligence in their classroom?

While each of these intelligences has its own distinct characteristics, we must remember that in Gardner's model the intelligences act in consort and are not mutually exclusive. Everyone has all the intelligences! Therefore, it's incorrect to label a child as a "kinesthetic learner" or a "verbal learner."

Rather, the model allows us as teachers to identify strengths in certain children and provide instructional opportunities that promote the development of all the intelligences in our students. MI theory was not developed to label or exclude individuals but to allow all learners to be successful through the different paths to learning that Gardner has identified. Also, while the intelligences function as distinct entities, there is a fair amount of overlap as we observe them operating in the classroom. They do not operate in isolation, even though we tend to discuss them in isolation when building an understanding of the theory.

Multiple Intelligences Survey

To appreciate the distribution of intelligences, it may help to administer an MI survey to your students. The completed sample survey in Table 1 is not a test but an inventory of learner preferences, a snapshot in time of how one student perceived her strengths in the nine categories.

Table 1

A Completed Multiple Intelligences Survey

	For each statement, enter a number one (1) if you agree with the statement or enjoy the activity being described. Enter a number zero (0) if you do not.	
Name:		**1 or 0**
EXAMPLE:	Swimming.	1
I like.....	Sorting things into groups.	1
	Thinking about life.	1
	Picturing things in my mind.	0
	Working with my hands.	1
	Studying patterns.	0
	Keeping things in order.	1
	Studying with a partner.	1
	Seeing how everything fits in the big picture.	0
	Learning a new language.	0
	Being right.	1
	Listening to sounds in nature.	1
	Moving around.	0
	Making up nonsense words.	0
	Following directions.	1
	Protecting nature.	0
	Decorating a room.	1
	Chatting online.	0
	Having strong feelings about things.	1
	Playing sports.	1
	Studying religion.	0
	Making art.	0

TABLE I ■ A COMPLETED MULTIPLE INTELLIGENCES SURVEY		
I like...	Moving to a beat.	0
	Writing stories.	1
	Solving problems.	0
	Completing a wordfind puzzle.	0
	Being on a team.	1
	Drawing maps.	1
	Hiking and camping.	0
	Playing an instrument.	0
	Practicing sign language.	1
	Studying art.	1
	Having things neat and tidy.	0
	Studying different countries.	0
	Being fair.	1
	Writing in a diary.	0
	Speaking up when I see something wrong.	1
	Rhyming words.	0
	Watching a play	0
	Working in a garden.	0
	Figuring out math problems.	0
	Being a good friend.	1
	Listening to music.	0
	Talking on the phone.	1
	Wondering about the universe.	0
	Exercising.	1
	Visiting national parks.	0
	Feeling good about my work.	0
	Remembering rhymes or words to songs.	0
	Creating graphs and charts.	1
	Making timelines.	0
	Having a debate.	1
	Getting along with others.	0
	Putting together a puzzle.	0
	Reading charts and tables.	0
	Making arts and crafts.	1
	Helping the poor.	0

TABLE I ■ A COMPLETED MULTIPLE INTELLIGENCES SURVEY		
I like...	Being with other people.	1
	Answering riddles.	1
	Watching a video.	0
	Writing letters.	1
	Dancing.	0
	Having background noise while I work.	1
	Working alone.	1
	Observing the stars and planets.	0
	Using my imagination.	1
	Knowing before something is about to happen.	1
	Learning about animals.	0
	Listening to all kinds of music.	0
	Using tools.	0
	Joining a club.	1
	Discussing why the world is the way it is.	1
	Being a leader.	1
	Giving a speech.	1
	Marching to a beat.	0
	Knowing why I should do something.	1
	Keeping things neat.	0
	Summarizing ideas.	1
	Building things.	0
	Recycling waste.	1
	Taking notes.	1
	Working with others.	0
	Planning things in my mind.	0
	Wondering about life on other planets.	1
	Being treated fairly.	0
	Going to the zoo.	1
	Making lists.	1
	Playing charades.	1
	Listening to a story.	0
	Reading books.	1
	Being around other people.	1
	Spending time outdoors.	1

The MI Survey is included as a Microsoft Excel spreadsheet with the filename MI_Survey on the CD-ROM that accompanies this book. Students can easily enter the data on the Inventory sheet by entering a "1" if they agree with the statement or enjoy the activity being described. They enter a "0" if they disagree with the statement or do not enjoy the activity being described.

After completing the survey, students can click the corresponding Scoring sheet tab to see their MI profile on the MI Survey Scoring Report (Figure 1). By highlighting the range of cells and clicking the Chart Wizard button, they can see a graphic representation of the profile. Be sure to discuss with your students the ways they can use this self-knowledge to help make the most of learning! Also on the CD-ROM is a color-coded version of the survey for teachers who wish to analyze survey items or break down student responses by intelligence (MI_Survey_Key).

The CD also includes a Primary Grades Multiple Intelligences Survey for nonreaders (a Microsoft Word file called MI_Survey_Primary). Print out and disseminate a copy to each student. Have students look at the set of 27 pictures and ask them to circle each image that represents an activity they like to do. Six of the images are shown in Figure 2.

It is possible that younger students may have difficulty recognizing what is going on in the pictures. A teacher administering the survey may have to explain the activity of each picture and ask students to circle the picture if they enjoy that activity. The Teacher Scoring Key on the CD-ROM (MI_Survey_Primary_Key) has captions under each picture describing the activity of the picture.

Figure 1. Sample of MI Survey Scoring Report

MI Survey Scoring Report

To graph your results, simply highlight the range B6:C22 and click on the Chart Wizard Button.

Verbal	4
Logical	3
Visual	4
Musical	7
Kinesthetic	7
Interpersonal	6
Intrapersonal	6
Naturalist	6
Existential	3

	% out of 30 items		proportion out of 100%
Analytic:	53%		35%
Interactive:	57%		37%
Introspective:	43%		28%
			out of
			100%

Strongest Domain: 57%

Figure 2. Sample from Primary MI Survey

Primary Grades Multiple Intelligences Survey

Circle each picture that shows an activity you like to do.

Student Name: _____

After your students have completed the inventory, you can use the key to quickly tally MI preferences. Some children may be inclined to circle most or all of the pictures in the survey. For these students, simply change the directions to have them place an X over each image they do not like to do. This will place students in a more critical mindset that will give you a better idea of their true preferences.

REMEMBER:

- Everyone has all the intelligences.
- You can strengthen an intelligence.
- This inventory is meant as a snapshot in time—it can change.
- MI is meant to empower people, not label them.

Are there more intelligences? There certainly may well be. Gardner tends to lean toward having a manageable group of broad categories rather than dozens and dozens of narrowly defined intelligences. In the case of the existential intelligence, for example, he was looking at a number of possible attributes for a "spiritualist" intelligence until he realized that if he backed up and looked at more general traits than just the spiritual he might be on to something much more identifiable and measurable. When he was done, he proposed the existential intelligence.

What other intelligences may yet be discovered? Gardner concedes he does not know, but he suggests that teachers may be a great source for suggested intelligences to research. After all, education is the one profession that dedicates its expertise to observing human learning and then diagnosing and prescribing instruction. What do you think might be a viable candidate as the next intelligence?

Relationships among the Intelligences

Having these basic definitions of each intelligence in place is important, but not as important as having a working understanding of how the intelligences relate to one another.

After all, if these different paths to learning always act in consort, we're really not providing for the full potential of this model unless we look at all of the intelligences in operation together. This can be difficult to do because once you begin observing a specific child the intelligences become very fluid and free flowing. What might be easily recognizable in isolation becomes much less clear when the intelligences are observed in action holistically.

For example, consider the student Chris, who is using her knowledge of simple machines to build a working model of a 6-inch by 2-inch car. She's working with two classmates at a learning center her teacher has prepared. Together the students have made a wooden chassis and placed axles and wheels in the appropriate places. This morning they are conducting test runs of their car down an inclined plane to see how adding weight to the chassis can improve the car's performance.

The critical question they are asking themselves is: "Where is the best place to add weight to the car in order to maximize its speed moving down an inclined plane?"

As an observer, which intelligences do you think you would see Chris using? Certainly the kinesthetic and interpersonal intelligences are evident. How about running the trials and recording the car speed based on the placement of weight? Is that more of a logical activity? Since the students are looking for patterns based on repeated trials, would this be a rhythmic task? And if they're creating a table that organizes their data so that they can make sense of their findings, wouldn't that be the naturalist intelligence? It's not so clear-cut once you begin observing learners in their environment!

When I present Gardner's theory to educators, they always come up with questions about this overlapping of intelligences. We are so accustomed to theory that nicely packages teaching and learning into neat compartments that we tend to cling to the individual integrity of each intelligence. It's hard to let go and accept the fact that, since Gardner's theory is based on the way these intelligences actually function within human cognition, it's a little less easy to compartmentalize and parcel them out in tight, tidy packages. Once teachers get

Figure 3. Wheel of MI Domains

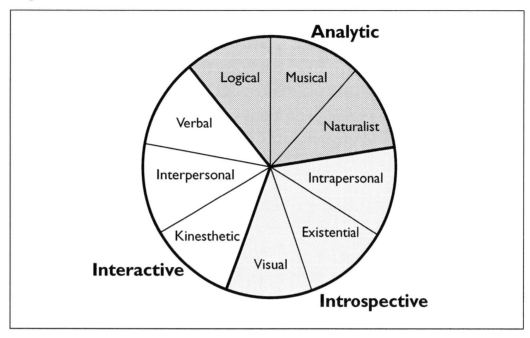

past the traditional definition of intelligence, they discover powerful new possibilities for learning in the classroom.

A Wheel of MI Domains

Consider the Wheel of MI Domains in Figure 3 for understanding the fluid relationship of the intelligences. First, I have grouped the intelligences into three regions, or domains: interactive, analytic, and introspective. These three domains are meant to align the intelligences with familiar learner attributes teachers routinely observe in the classroom.

The Interactive Domain

The interactive domain consists of the verbal, interpersonal, and kinesthetic intelligences. Learners typically employ these intelligences to express themselves and explore their environment.

Consider 5-year-old Dan in his kindergarten classroom. He not only uses language to demonstrate his knowledge and express his needs, he also uses it to explore, inquire, and prompt responses from others. This can include the use of nonsensical expressions, repetitive recountings of favorite books, and even reversion to "baby talk." Regardless of the many functions of language Dan uses, he consistently uses talk to interact with others and his environment.

Eleven-year-old Miranda provides a prime example of the interactive function of the interpersonal intelligence. As her class reads E.G. Speare's *The Witch of Blackbird Pond* she continually prompts her teacher to ask about the mores of 17th-century New England. Miranda initiates class discussion on the social dynamics of prosecuting witches in Colonial New England, not for the sake of the discussion itself but to help her better understand the plot and setting of the story. When it comes time to be assessed for comprehension of the novel, Miranda excels in an interview format, in which she can discuss her understandings and ideas at length. In fact, her teacher offers several assessment options, including the opportunity to have a classmate interview her as the heroine from the book.

Finally, consider Lin's use of her kinesthetic intelligence as an interactive process. Lin has been learning about electrical circuits in her third-grade class. This week the teacher has set up an experiment as a learning center in which Lin and her classmates must use batteries, copper wiring, and light bulbs to create electrical circuits. Lin and her group of three classmates quickly create a complete circuit. They then ask their teacher, Mrs. Morales, for some paper clips so that they can experiment making a switch that will open and close the circuit. Finally Lin's group takes the experiment a step further by creating a parallel circuit using two light bulbs. Lin has repeatedly interacted with her environment and her peers to create a greater understanding of how electrical circuits work.

I characterize these three intelligences as interactive because even though they can be stimulated through passive activity they typically invite and encourage interaction to achieve understanding. Even if students complete a task individually, they must consider others through the way they write, create, construct, and arrive at conclusions. The interactive intelligences are by nature social processes.

The Analytic Domain

The analytic domain consists of the logical, musical, and naturalist intelligences, which promote the learner's analysis of knowledge.

Consider Ms. Melinski's class. Her students have created instruments that simulate the sounds of the rainforest, and the children are now using these sounds to create their own individual compositions. As the children come before the class to present and conduct their compositions, they must follow the patterns of sound and imitate them accurately to successfully perform the piece. There is a careful auditory analysis of each rhythm presented to the class, and in cases where the student has created sheet music with symbols for playing the different instruments, there is visual analysis of patterns as well.

The logical intelligence has a highly analytical component. Consider Uri and Celeste, who are creating a bridge out of Popsicle sticks that will be able to hold the weight of a motorized 12-pound truck crossing the structure. They have studied many kinds of bridges and are employing what they have learned to make their structure strong enough to successfully do the job. As they attempt different designs, they are careful to analyze their failures and build on their successes. After 2 weeks of working a little every day, Uri and Celeste come up with a design that safely holds the truck's weight. Problem solving is a very analytical process!

Finally, consider Suzanne, who, in a first-grade learning center, is sorting leaves by different attributes. She sorts them by color, then by size, then by texture. As she comes up with a leaf classification system that makes sense to her, she glues each leaf to a large sheet of paper that serves as an organizer. She then presents her leaf classification system to be displayed in the classroom so that other children can compare and contrast their own strategies for classification with Suzanne's.

I characterize these three intelligences as analytic because even though they can have a social or introspective component, they most fundamentally promote the process of analyzing and incorporating data into existing schema. The analytic intelligences are by nature heuristic processes.

The Introspective Domain

The introspective domain consists of the existential, intrapersonal, and visual intelligences. These are the intelligences that have a distinctly affective component. In the case of the visual intelligence, consider Michelangelo celebrating the discovery of a large slab of marble from which he wants to free the angel encased therein through his act of sculpting.

There is a uniquely emotional component to envisioning a piece of art before the artist actually creates it. For example, recall a student you have worked with who served as a class leader simply because he or she was able to visualize where to go with a project before the rest of the group even got its collective self together to begin discussing the possibilities. There is an intuitive release of energy that sparks the enthusiasm and imagination of others when the visual intelligence is unleashed. The existential intelligence displays similar emotional, introspective characteristics.

When Soeren Kierkegaard described looking at the infinite depth of the night sky and having an emotionally charged response that said, "Yes, I am part of something bigger in the universe!" he was referring to this experience. It is necessary to make that leap of faith in order to contribute to the collective human experience.

For instance, place yourself in the presence of the Pieta and feel the emotional response as your senses take in the aesthetic beauty of one of humanity's great expressions of human love and suffering. It moves many unsuspecting onlookers to tears. This is another example of the emotional response to cognitive stimulus.

The intrapersonal intelligence may be the most obvious example of this. Consider 14-year-old Kristin, who filters everything she learns through her strong sense of social justice. She lights up when she learns about the plight of Native Americans in the 19th century, or discovers the ethical dilemmas presented by genetic engineering, or reads Alan Paton's *Cry, the Beloved Country*. Not surprisingly, with an upcoming presidential election in the fall, Kristin becomes very interested in helping out at her local party headquarters and campaigning for the candidates of her choice. Everything Kristin learns is reinforced and mastered by the emotional connection she has with the different kinds of content she studies.

I characterize these three intelligences as introspective because they require the learner to look inward and they require an emotive connection to the learner's own experiences and beliefs in order to make sense of new learning. The introspective intelligences are by nature affective processes.

Using the Wheel of MI Domains

By using the Wheel of MI Domains, you can begin to get a handle on the nature of the various intelligences based on their primary process as evidenced in the classroom. This is not to say that these domains represent hard-and-fast categories. All the intelligences still act in consort. Just as the example of bridge building can be seen as a strongly logical activity, it obviously requires interpersonal, verbal, kinesthetic, visual, and even musical and naturalist components. The wheel offers a balance in planning the stimulation of the different intelligences, while at the same time bringing all the intelligences together at its center point.

Consider using the wheel to select one intelligence from each domain in planning a lesson. This offers a balance among the three and the potential for a well-rounded lesson with regard to the intelligences.

For example, a teacher's lesson on Shakespeare's soliloquies may benefit from having students use the verbal (interactive), musical (analytic), and existential (introspective) intelligences. By tapping into all three ways of knowing, the lesson accommodates the learners who respond to the soliloquies. The diagrammed version of the lesson might look like this:

- **Objective:** Given a soliloquy selected from *Macbeth*, the learner will recite the soliloquy with proper meter and correctly interpret its content.

- **Intelligences:**

  VERBAL—recitation of the soliloquy

  MUSICAL—knowledge of the soliloquy's meter

  EXISTENTIAL—interpretation of the sentiment expressed in the soliloquy

The teacher is now ready to develop the procedure and assessment for the lesson based on the use of the Wheel of MI Domains.

Then again, a teacher may decide to target one domain in a lesson and select two or three intelligences from the same domain in order to bolster the learning experience for students. In having students dissect earthworms, a teacher may want to emphasize the analytical nature of the task and decide to map to the logical, musical, and naturalist intelligences in this lesson. Here is the diagrammed version of the lesson:

- **Objective:** Given an earthworm to dissect, the learner will follow specific step-by-step instructions, categorizing organs by body systems and identifying patterns found within those systems.

- **Intelligences:**

  LOGICAL—following sequential directions

  MUSICAL—identifying patterns within the body structure

  NATURALIST—categorizing organs by body system

The Wheel of MI Domains can be a helpful tool in creating lessons that are balanced and targeted with regard to the distribution of intelligences in your classroom.

Reflections

1 How did the intelligences distribute in your classroom based on the MI survey? Which were the top three intelligence scores for your class? Which were the bottom three scores?

2 How can the information you gathered from the MI survey be used in future instruction?

3 When is it most appropriate to plan for the use of intelligences in the same domain on the wheel? When is it most appropriate to plan for the use of intelligences from different domains? Why?

Chapter 3

Technology and Multiple Intelligences

Over the years technology has flooded the field of education with many promises made on many dollars spent. We as teachers have manned the trenches as hardware, software, and best practices have poured into our classrooms with the explicit understanding that they were to bolster teaching and learning. Ask any one of us what our experience has been with technology, though, and we will tell you of victories and struggles, good intentions and naive assumptions, all woven together in a tapestry of hits and misses.

Now that we are being asked to account for that spending and the impact it has had on learning, it seems painfully obvious that we have to rethink our priorities in integrating technology into instruction. Education needs leaders who will help set those priorities.

Crafting Technology Standards

The International Society for Technology in Education (ISTE) has developed a set of six National Educational Technology Standards (NETS) for Students to help teachers harness the power of technology in their instructional planning. The standards were developed not only to promote learning through effective uses of technology but also to foster those 21st-century job skills that will be in such demand.

There are six broad categories with descriptive standards within each. Each standard is written to help us keep our sights on the proper priorities in implementing instructional technology. Note how ISTE's standards match up with Gardner's intelligences in considering appropriate student uses of technology.

ISTE NETS for Students Compared to Gardner's Intelligences

1. BASIC OPERATIONS AND CONCEPTS

- Students demonstrate a sound understanding of the nature and operation of technology systems.

    Logical, naturalist—explain the organization of different systems and how they function.

- Students are proficient in the use of technology.

    Kinesthetic—manipulate different technologies, both industrial and digital, for goal-oriented tasks.

2. SOCIAL, ETHICAL, AND HUMAN ISSUES

- Students understand the ethical, cultural, and societal issues related to technology.

> **Intrapersonal, existential**—understand and internalize the individual and communal values for technology use.

- Students practice responsible use of technology systems, information, and software.

  > **Intrapersonal, existential**—put into practice the internalization of individual and communal values for technology use.

- Students develop positive attitudes toward technology uses that support life-long learning, collaboration, personal pursuits, and productivity.

  > **Intrapersonal, existential**—develop attitudes that will promote technology use that will improve the quality of life.

3. TECHNOLOGY PRODUCTIVITY TOOLS

- Students use technology tools to enhance learning, increase productivity, and promote creativity.

  > **Verbal, kinesthetic, visual**—use technology to apply learning in new and different ways.

- Students use productivity tools to collaborate in constructing technology-enhanced models, prepare publications, and produce other creative works.

  > **Verbal, kinesthetic, interpersonal, visual**—participate in teams to apply learning in new and different ways.

4. TECHNOLOGY COMMUNICATIONS TOOLS

- Students use telecommunications to collaborate, publish, and interact with peers, experts, and other audiences.

  > **Verbal, interpersonal**—virtually interact with one another in completing goal-oriented tasks.

- Students use a variety of media and formats to communicate information and ideas effectively to multiple audiences.

  > **Verbal, musical, interpersonal**—use the varied affordances of technology to demonstrate learning to others.

5. TECHNOLOGY RESEARCH TOOLS

- Students use technology to locate, evaluate, and collect information from a variety of sources.

  > **Verbal, logical, naturalist, intrapersonal**—access, categorize, and evaluate information for specific tasks.

- Students use technology tools to process data and report results.

  > **Verbal, logical, musical, naturalist**—format research results in clean, organized, well-developed presentations.

- Students evaluate and select new information resources and technological innovations based on the appropriateness for specific tasks.

  Intrapersonal, naturalist—analyze data and technologies within the context of an assigned task to determine their value.

6. TECHNOLOGY PROBLEM-SOLVING AND DECISION-MAKING TOOLS

- Students use technology resources for solving problems and making informed decisions.

  Logical, intrapersonal, existential—use technology to make appropriate choices based on the data provided.

- Students employ technology in the development of strategies for solving problems in the real world.

  Logical, intrapersonal, existential—use technology to generate effective solutions to problems that can improve the quality of life.

ISTE NETS for Students addresses all of Gardner's intelligences in broad, well-rounded categories. By using these standards as guidelines for planning technology use in your classroom, building, and school, you can help ensure that instruction accommodates a number of intelligences and technologies. With the standards as a firm foundation on which we can build, let's take a closer look at the different kinds of technologies available in the classroom.

Industrial Technologies

What comes to mind when you think of technology? If you were born before the last quarter of the 20th century you will no doubt conjure up images of construction sites, factories, and farm machinery. These were familiar sights long before the advent of computers. Industrial technologies provided a breakthrough in our ability to do work, to use machines and engines to create goods and provide services more efficiently and economically. They transformed the world from an exclusively agricultural economy to an industrial marketplace, bringing nations and cultures closer together over time.

Still, human expertise was necessary for Industrial Age tools to be used productively. The workers' roles on assembly lines became more specialized, but it wasn't until fairly recently that assembly lines could be made to function exclusively through robotics. And even now, when the line goes down due to some mechanical failure, experts need to troubleshoot and repair the problem. The human variable still comes into play.

Because industrial technologies tend to be hands-on, they remain very useful in classroom instruction. Educators have become highly aware of the use of manipulative materials in promoting learning and understanding. From the Language Experience Approach and Math Their Way to Problem-Based Instruction and Learning Laboratories, education is replete with examples of learning as a multisensory, interactive process. Industrial technologies were developed to simplify real-world applications for humankind, and they helped bring those real-world applications into the classroom for students.

Industrial Technologies and Education

Perhaps the best example of an early industrial technology is the chalkboard. Imagine the breakthrough for educators that occurred when a chalkboard could be mounted on a wall where it could be cleaned and reused daily. No longer was it necessary for individual hand-held slate boards to be distributed to the entire class.

Here also was a new focal point for the classroom, when all written communication could be shared with the class at one time. Teachers no longer had to disseminate all information orally, nor did they have to present written lessons individually or in small, huddled groups. Suddenly the classroom seemed more open, and everyone had breathing room to work individually.

Now jump ahead a century and consider the effect the overhead projector had on instruction. The chalkboard was by then commonplace in the classroom, with its chalk dust and daily cleaning chores. The overhead projector allowed teachers the same convenience of presenting material to the entire room by writing on a reusable surface. The big breakthrough was that teachers could now write assignments on an overhead and never have to turn their backs on the class. Instruction became more engaged and engaging, with brightly colored transparencies that caught students' attention and provided better explanations of material in greater visual detail. In some classrooms the inception of the overhead projector relegated the chalkboard to a place for magnets and a projection screen.

While technologies like these may have been designed specifically for instructional purposes, many industrial technologies were not developed specifically for education but have nonetheless been integrated into the classroom to facilitate learning. Look in any science laboratory and you will see an inventory of all kinds of equipment adapted for use in instruction: beakers, Bunsen burners, safety goggles, syringes, batteries, measuring tapes, and faucets for running water, to name a few.

Consider the tools used in vocational education programs for auto repair, woodworking, and cooking. The tools of each trade are Industrial Age technologies that are necessary for hands-on apprenticeship at the high school level. From elementary grades on up, technology is all around us in the classroom. Any innovation designed by humans to help us more effectively interact with our environment is potentially an educational technology.

Unfortunately, many industrial technologies have always been limited to alternative education programs. For the mainstream classroom, lecture, reading and writing, and computation have been the staples of education. Introducing real-world technologies has been perceived as a necessity only for those students who could not function in an environment built around the linguistic and logical intelligences. As we have learned more through brain research, though, classroom learning environments have become less centered on linguistic or logical factors and have become more inclusive of technologies that can stimulate all the known paths to learning.

Industrial Technologies and MI Theory

Gardner's MI theory is significant in that it gives teachers a framework in which they can identify the appropriate uses of industrial technologies for instruction. Whereas child-centered teachers may have always instinctively included opportunities for building and creating in the classroom, they may now incorporate these activities with a greater confidence because they accommodate inclusive kinds and qualities of learning. The integration of industrial technologies into the classroom need no longer be a hit-or-miss proposition!

The first step in using technology effectively in the classroom is to apply our knowledge of different technologies to Gardner's model. For example, using a lever on simple machines in a science unit at first glance stimulates the kinesthetic path to learning. However, depending on the intended use of the lever in a lesson, it can stimulate a number of other intelligences. For example, if the student is expected to determine the correct placement of a fulcrum to lift a textbook off a table using the least amount of energy, the logical intelligence comes into play. Then again, if students are asked to identify the kinds of levers in use around the classroom it becomes an exercise in logical, musical, and naturalist intelligences as they look for patterns and classify levers by their attributes. The intelligences a technology stimulates are dictated by the context in which the technology is used for instruction.

With this in mind, let's consider how different nondigital technologies map to each of the intelligences, as shown in Table 2. While this mapping is by no means exhaustive, it does offer some examples of nondigital technologies and the intelligences they stimulate.

By keeping in mind the affordances of each technology, teachers can successfully select those industrial applications that will match learning objectives to the intelligences that thrive in every classroom. For example, in teaching about ancient Greece, teachers may already use lots of verbal and visual technologies. However, they can expand their students' study by including these technologies in the unit:

- Use hands-on materials to apply the principles developed by ancient Greek mathematicians (Logical/Mathematical)

- Construct working models of simple machines used in daily life in ancient Greece (Bodily/Kinesthetic)

- Record a tape of the sounds that would be heard on the streets of ancient Athens, with each student contributing to the recording (Musical/Rhythmic)

- Create fictional journals in which each student shares his or her reactions to events that occurred in ancient Greece (Intrapersonal)

- Design costumes and participate in an improvisation related to an important event in Greek history (Interpersonal/Existential)

Table 2

Intelligences and Nondigital Technologies

INTELLIGENCE	NONDIGITAL TECHNOLOGIES
VERBAL/LINGUISTIC	Pencil, pen, worksheets, textbooks, newspaper, magazine, typewriter, microphone
MATHEMATICAL/LOGICAL	Cuisenaire rods, unifix cubes, tangrams, measuring cups, measuring scales, ruler/yardstick, slide rule, calculator
VISUAL/SPATIAL	Picture books, art supplies, chalkboard, dry erase board, overhead projector, slide projector, TV/VCR, camera, video camera
BODILY/KINESTHETIC	Construction tools, kitchen utensils, screw, lever, wheel and axle, inclined plane, pulley, wedge, physical education equipment
MUSICAL/RHYTHMICAL	Pattern blocks, puzzles, musical instruments, phonograph, headphones, tape player/recorder
INTRAPERSONAL	Journals, diaries, surveys, voting machines, learning centers, children's literature
INTERPERSONAL	Post-it notes, greeting cards, laboratory, telephone, walkie-talkie, intercom, mail, board games, costumes
NATURALIST	Magnifying glass, microscope, telescope, bug box, scrap book, sandwich bag, plastic container
EXISTENTIAL	Art replica, planetarium, stage drama, classic literature, classic philosophy, symbols of world religions, simulation games

- Prepare Greek foods and categorize them based on their taste or ingredients (Kinesthetic/Naturalist)

- Conduct a classroom planetarium by devising constellation projections using flashlights and container lids (Kinesthetic/Existential)

By accommodating a variety of intelligences in your instruction, you can increase your students' opportunities for comprehension, retention, and recall of material, whether you are building your students' long-term understanding or preparing them for standardized testing.

Digital Technologies

The last 30 years have changed the landscape of technology and, indeed, society. The advent of the microcomputer introduced a whole new level of opportunity to effectively and efficiently interact with our environment. Early on, the emphasis was on peripherals that would help us use the microcomputer to accomplish traditional tasks. Light pens, touch pads, and touch screens were meant to allow us to input information to the computer using familiar utensils. At the same time, the software that was developed was linear in nature, favoring word-processing, math, and science applications over more open-ended activities. Simulations had their place in science and social studies software, but the applications tended to be limited by the technology of the time.

Productivity packages offered a different approach to technology use. The combination of word-processing, spreadsheet, database, and multimedia production software in one suite of digital tools allowed users to apply software to their unique needs. For example, a small business could use a productivity package to keep track of its expenses, profits, and clients.

With a little ingenuity, tax records, invoices, and contracts could also be managed using a software suite. However, the way a software application suite is used in a classroom is very different from the way it is used in a small business. Students can use word processing and spreadsheets to create and augment research papers and reports using data they have gathered. Databases can be used to track each student's reading throughout the year or to create mailing labels for a long-term project that requires partners in other parts of the world.

Moreover, no one has more fun with multimedia production software than students as they experiment with new and different ways to present what they have learned. Productivity packages are much more versatile and adaptable than software titles developed around specific content or tasks.

The explosion in the development of the Internet is probably the single most important event that ushered in of Digital Age. From electronic mail and gophers to file transfer protocol, synchronous communication, and the World Wide Web, the Internet has made digital technology as vital and immediate as the industrial technologies that preceded it. No longer can computers be expected to belong solely in the domain of business or to be used solely by math and science scholars. Now everyone can communicate and access data using a phone line. The limits of time and space in the Industrial Age were erased with single keystrokes, and everyone can now appreciate how the new computer technologies exponentially improved the quality of life at work, school, and home. Today, when you say the word "technology" to individuals born since 1980, they immediately conjure up images of Web sites, instant messaging, and electronic mail.

Digital Technologies and Education

As schools try to change with society and provide students with the skills they will need to compete in the job market in the Digital Age, they have purchased the hardware and infrastructure necessary to begin integrating digital technology into the industrial classroom. Labs have been set up and acceptable use policies have been put in place to promote the use of these new technologies. Software has been purchased and local area networks have been built to try to keep up with the quickly changing digital world. Schools are truly on the technology bandwagon.

But where is that bandwagon headed, and how willing are teachers to stay on for the ride if there isn't a sound educational destination? Technology for technology's sake has a shine that quickly loses its luster. School systems have stashes of hardware and software that are no longer in use because they didn't live up to their billing. That, coupled with quickly changing technology, makes investing in digital technology seem like a very risky business.

The only way to ensure that technologies purchased and implemented will be successful in the classroom is to make sure they are well grounded in instructional and learning theory, thoughtfully implemented, and then reflected upon. And no theory is more capable of matching technology to learners than Gardner's model. Consider how the digital technologies listed in Table 3 map to each of the nine intelligences.

Table 3

Intelligences and Digital Technologies

INTELLIGENCE	DIGITAL TECHNOLOGIES
VERBAL/LINGUISTIC	Keyboard, electronic mail, speech recognition devices, text bridges
MATHEMATICAL/LOGICAL	Graphing calculators, FTP clients, gophers, search engines
VISUAL/SPATIAL	Monitor, digital camera/camcorder, scanner
BODILY/KINESTHETIC	Mouse, joystick, assistive technologies
MUSICAL/RHYTHMICAL	Speakers, CD-ROM disks, CD-ROM players
INTRAPERSONAL	Online forms, real-time projects
INTERPERSONAL	Chat, message boards, instant messengers
NATURALIST	Floppy drive, file manager, semantic mapping tools
EXISTENTIAL	MUVEs, virtual reality, virtual communities, simulations

Later we will identify specific kinds of software that stimulate the different intelligences. By mapping available technologies to the nine intelligences, we can maximize the effectiveness of our use of technology in instruction.

How can digital technology stimulate the intelligences? The process is not usually as hands-on as with the Industrial Age technologies. Consider how the teacher Tronie Gunn developed a unit for her students on sorting and searching using spreadsheets. Table 4 shows how she is able to address eight of the nine intelligences using a specially structured lesson plan format that allows her to carefully map each element of her lesson to the appropriate intelligences.

In this lesson students learn to sort data in different ways, and then determine from the results of their work which ways of sorting the data are the most efficient.

Teachers can modify this lesson to use sorting strategies that are most appropriate for their students. The goal is to help children experience the most useful and efficient ways of looking at data via technology.

Notice how Tronie's selection of technologies is consistent with the intelligences she wanted to stimulate through this lesson. Her objective is succinctly stated and the intelligences are clearly indicated in framing the context for the software and hardware she intends to use. The instructional design of the lesson provides the

Table 4
"Sorting and Searching" Lesson

LESSON TITLE: Sorting and Searching GRADE LEVEL: 10		TEACHER: Tronie Gunn Westbury High School Houston, Texas	
SUBJECT(S):	DATE: October 17, 2001	TIME: Two 1-hour periods	
OBJECTIVE(S): Using a spreadsheet, the learners will test standard filters using varied sets of data, comparing each sort for its time and space efficiency.	**INTELLIGENCES:** Verbal Logical Visual Interpersonal Intrapersonal Kinesthetic	**TECHNOLOGIES:** Computer lab (Pentium 3 computers), spreadsheet	**NETS FOR STUDENTS:** 1. Students demonstrate a sound understanding of the nature and operation of technology systems.
MATERIALS: Sorting and Algorithmic Analysis worksheet (see below), overhead transparencies and an erasable marker, playing cards		**INTELLIGENCES:** Verbal, Logical, Visual, Interpersonal, Intrapersonal, Kinesthetic	
PROCEDURE: *Prelesson Class Preparation:* Students read textbook chapter which describes a variety of sorting algorithms that can be used in a spreadsheet. Students have previously used Excel. Lesson: 1. Provide a brief review/overview (use a computer projector when applicable) of the 10 kinds of sorts students will study and compare, the types and sizes of data that will be used, and the investigation tools provided. Based on this overview, students will be allowed to select their preferred sort for investigation (first-come-first-serve)		**INTELLIGENCES:** Verbal Verbal Visual Naturalist Intrapersonal	

TABLE 4 ■ "SEARCHING AND SORTING" LESSON	
PROCEDURE:	**INTELLIGENCES:**
2. Assign each student a different sort to investigate individually using the resources provided (you may assign a sort to more than one student if your class size dictates). Students may use these three resources to conduct their investigation:	Visual Musical Naturalist
Teach Yourself Data Structures and Algorithms CD—provides examples of most of the sorts (in fast or slow motion and for different kinds of data)	Visual Musical Naturalist
Exposure Supplementary Materials CD—provides visual demonstrations for most of the sorts (using dots or bars)	Logical Musical Naturalist
Exposure CD—provides a program in chapter 43 that allows a detailed investigation of each of the identified sorts, specifying different types of data and providing the elapsed time required to complete the sort	Logical Kinesthetic
3. Each student builds an Excel spreadsheet for the algorithm studied. If more than one student investigated a given algorithm, average the results.	Logical Musical Naturalist
Use playing cards to demonstrate a working knowledge of how each sort works.	Kinesthetic Musical
Reflect on why some sorts do not work for some data.	Intrapersonal Musical
4. Use an overhead projector and transparencies to report results of the investigations and to facilitate comparisons of the different algorithms.	Interpersonal Logical Musical Naturalist
ASSESSMENT:	**INTELLIGENCES:**
Completed worksheet	Verbal Logical
Demonstration with playing cards	Kinesthetic
Class discussion	Interpersonal Intrapersonal

context for the intelligences she selects, and the intelligences dictate the appropriate technologies. Notice too that she uses both digital and traditional media in her lesson. Her students can look forward to a challenging, stimulating immersion into the world of spreadsheet filters.

Reflections

1 How can the ISTE NETS for Students help you to develop well-grounded, technology-based instruction?

2 How does the instructional context help you to determine the intelligences a technology will stimulate?

3 Which domains on the MI wheel did Tronie emphasize in her lesson?

Chapter 4

Media Selection

Teachers are avid consumers of all kinds of media. Different media are always in the classroom, and they affect the quality and success of instruction. A lesson presented several times using various media will look different each time it is observed. This is because as consumers of information we screen everything we take in through the medium in which it is conveyed. The medium used in a learning context is, in fact, part of the learning experience. As MI practitioners we already subscribe to an experiential learning model, but how explicitly aware are we of the impact instructional media have on learning?

Instructional Media

While visiting with teachers from different parts of the country, I often discuss the current state of technology in their buildings. And regardless of their circumstances, one common denominator surfaces as we talk. Teachers feel bound by their access to technology regardless of what it may be. If a teacher has access to a television connected to her computer so that she can introduce new content via group instruction, then that is what she will do. Then again, if she has an LCD projector and a demonstration station at the front of a fully equipped lab, she'll be more likely to use that set-up rather than the TV. But not many classrooms are that well endowed with technology. Educators have a long and storied history of making the most of what they've got. There are still teachers making do very well with MECC software in an Apple II GS lab, thank you. Yes, the technology is 20 years old, but it's what they have to work with. Teachers make do.

Most of us lie somewhere between 20-year-old technology and today's cutting-edge digital tools. We have choices. Not every lesson needs to make use of what is most familiar to us. Yes, the overhead projector and a TV/VCR combination will get a workout in most any school. What about the laserdisc library? Most teachers aren't familiar or comfortable enough with it to make it part of their regular instruction. How about spreadsheets and databases? Yes, they are installed on most machines, but many teachers haven't used them routinely in the classroom because they're just not comfortable enough with their own proficiency to do so. Access, comfort level, and training are all important factors in changing this reality.

MI theory serves as an impetus to challenge the status quo. Once we subscribe to Gardner's theory, we have bought into the premise that we are teaching children, not books and not curriculum. With this conviction firmly in place it becomes imperative that we look at the different ways we reach children. Traditional media, such as textbooks, are simply not enough. There was a time in this country's history when we taught the textbook. Today we teach the children. And as we become more aware of the different modalities through which we learn, we are in ever more need of ways to accommodate all the different learners in our classrooms.

Fifty years ago this would have been a formidable challenge. But this is the Information Age, and we have technology developing at exponential rates that helps us meet the needs of all learners. It is truly an amazing time to be in education because the results of brain research and technology meld to help reinforce the conviction that all children can learn.

Media and Intelligences

What are the different media and methodologies we have at our disposal? Think about all the different ways you provide learning experiences for your learners. From the beginning of the morning through afternoon dismissal, how do you create instruction for your students? Here is a list of media you may use on any given day:

- Textbook
- Pencil and paper
- Chalkboard
- Overhead projector
- Manipulatives
- Television
- Video
- Tape player/tape recorder
- Magazines
- Newspaper

These are common tools introduced to the classroom over the centuries as technology has made it possible. With the dawn of the Digital Age, there is an entirely new set of tools.

- CD player
- Laserdisc
- Word processing
- Desktop publishing
- Multimedia presentations
- Spreadsheets
- Databases
- Digital References
- Electronic mail
- Web sites
- Newsgroups
- Mailing lists
- Collaborative projects
- Virtual environments

The variety of media available to educators today truly is impressive. The question, though, is not just one of access but of appropriateness. Given that we have more choices today, how do we select the most appropriate media for the learning task at hand? Media selection is a vital piece of instructional design that is often overlooked when implementing a lesson.

Selecting the Media

To make appropriate media selection, you must first look at your learners. Are they being introduced to new material, are they practicing skills or concepts, or are they reviewing content already taught? What background material have they already covered? Are there prerequisite skills they need to master? What is their ability level with the instructional content?

Second, look at the learning objective. Is it appropriate for your learners? What is to be accomplished by the end of this lesson? How have you structured activities to make this possible? How will you evaluate learner success at the end of the lesson? By answering these four questions you can identify which technologies will match your identified objective. This helps you to narrow down your media choices for the lesson.

Finally, consider the intelligences. Which of the nine will you stimulate in this lesson? Are there additional intelligences from the MI wheel that would help balance your instruction? Which technologies best accommodate these intelligences? Answering these questions will help you lock in the technology or technologies that are appropriate for your lesson.

The process flows accordingly:

Learner ⟶ Objective ⟶ Intelligences ⟶ Technology

By considering instructional design factors in this order, you can successfully select appropriate media for any lesson in your classroom.

Supporting Intelligences with Technology

Considering the learner and objective will be second nature to most teachers. But how do we consider the intelligences with regard to technology? It is tempting to select the technology you want to use and then make it "fit" the intelligences. However, does that process truly help you identify appropriate strategies, or does it simply let you go through the motions to justify your personal preferences? Instead, start with your knowledge of intelligences and consider which media will naturally support them. Table 5 gives some examples.

Let's take a closer look at each intelligence and the media that offer appropriate support.

THE VERBAL/LINGUISTIC INTELLIGENCE, always well accommodated in the classroom, can be even more effectively supported through modern technologies. Set aside the traditional textbook, pencil, and paper and consider the ways word processing promotes not only composition but also editing and revising in ways that streamline the Writer's Workshop approach. Desktop publishing and Web-based publishing take this idea to new levels of efficacy because students can see their work celebrated within the classroom and beyond in the "virtual" world. Electronic mail is a wonderful way to promote verbal/linguistic learning because students are prompted to inquire of and respond to correspondents through written text.

Table 5

Intelligences and Technologies

INTELLIGENCE	TECHNOLOGIES
VERBAL/LINGUISTIC	Textbook, pencil, worksheet, newspaper, magazine, word processing, electronic mail, desktop publishing, Web-based publishing, keyboard, speech recognition devices, text bridges
MATHEMATICAL/LOGICAL	Lecture, Cuisenaire rods, unifix cubes, tangrams, measuring cups, measuring scales, ruler/yardstick, slide rule, graphing calculators, spreadsheet, search engine, directory, FTP clients, gophers, WebQuests, problem-solving tasks, programming languages
VISUAL/SPATIAL	Overhead projector, television, video, picture books, art supplies, chalkboard, dry erase board, slideshows, charting and graphing, monitor, digital camera/camcorder, scanner, graphics editor, HTML editor, digital animation/movies
BODILY/KINESTHETIC	Construction tools, kitchen utensils, screw, lever, wheel and axle, inclined plane, pulley, wedge, physical education equipment, manipulative materials, mouse, joystick, simulations that require eye-hand coordination, assistive technologies
MUSICAL/RHYTHMICAL	Pattern blocks, puzzles, musical instruments, phonograph, headphones, tape player/recorder, digital sounds, online pattern games, multimedia presentations, speakers, CD–ROM disks, CD–ROM player
INTRAPERSONAL	Journals, diaries, surveys, voting machines, learning centers, children's literature, class debate, real-time projects, online surveys, online forms, digital portfolios with self-assessments
INTERPERSONAL	Class discussion, Post-it notes, greeting cards, laboratory, telephone, walkie-talkie, intercom, board games, costumes, collaborative projects, chat rooms, message boards, instant messenger
NATURALIST	Magnifying glass, microscope, telescope, bug box, scrap book, sandwich bag, plastic container database, laserdisc, floppy drive, file manager, semantic mapping tools
EXISTENTIAL	Art replica, planetarium, stage drama, classic literature, classic philosophy, symbols of world religions, virtual communities, virtual art exhibits, virtual field trips, MUDs, virtual reality, simulations

THE LOGICAL/MATHEMATICAL INTELLIGENCE is promoted through activities that stimulate reasoning. These activities can include a traditional lecture, analyzing data through a spreadsheet, conducting queries using a search engine or directory, participating in the problem-solving process of a WebQuest, and even mastering a programming language or a networked system of computers.

THE VISUAL/SPATIAL INTELLIGENCE especially benefits from technology in modern education because there are so many new ways to stimulate this path to learning. While the overhead projector, slide projector, and TV/VCR have been around for 30 years or more, the use of digital slideshows is a newer way to create, manipulate, and present learning in the classroom. All kinds of applications (word processors, draw/paint programs, spreadsheets, databases) have made charting and graphing so much easier than it was in days gone by, and graphics editors now allow us to manipulate any image to meet our needs. Throw in the possibilities for Web site design and construction and the recent advances in digital animation and movies and you can easily see why the visual/spatial intelligence is so aptly supported by technology.

THE BODILY/KINESTHETIC INTELLIGENCE is stimulated by physical interaction with one's environment. When technology is used in instruction, students who manipulate materials can develop a greater understanding of skills and concepts. Diagramming on the board, sorting manipulative materials by attributes, participating in a group simulation, or using an adaptive switch to input responses into a computer are all examples of how the bodily/kinesthetic intelligence can be accommodated.

THE MUSICAL/RHYTHMIC INTELLIGENCE is the intelligence of patterns. Technology accommodates it in a variety of ways. For example, using a tape player and following along with books in a listening center prompts the use of this intelligence. Incorporating digital sounds into a multimedia presentation also accommodates this path to learning. Playing online pattern games like Mastermind and Concentration can support the musical/rhythmic intelligence. Even looking for visual patterns in the classroom or schoolyard fosters musical/rhythmic thinking.

THE INTRAPERSONAL INTELLIGENCE is stimulated through activities that bring feelings, values, and attitudes into play. For example, conducting a class debate on an environmental issue, following a real-time expedition through uncharted islands, completing online surveys on an issue being studied in the classroom, completing an online form as a facilitating event for a unit of study, or evaluating one's own digital portfolio full of work from a semester or marking period are all good ways to nurture the intrapersonal intelligence.

THE INTERPERSONAL INTELLIGENCE can be accommodated through class discussion on relevant topics, collaborative projects that enrich and extend the curriculum, synchronous chat among groups of students or with experts, participation in newsgroups on an assigned topic, and even mailing lists that allow multiple classes to share ideas and experiences asynchronously.

THE NATURALIST INTELLIGENCE is stimulated by organizing and making sense of information in categories and hierarchies. Creating a database to sort and search through data is a wonderful naturalist exercise. Using a laserdisc on weather is an effective way to share scientific phenomena in the classroom. More than any other activity, though, semantic mapping is decidedly the most naturalist. Consider the use of the software application Inspiration in visually mapping out understandings of facts and concepts and how it allows the learner to manipulate ideas.

THE EXISTENTIAL INTELLIGENCE is stimulated through learning experiences that reinforce one's sense of being and feeling part of something greater than one's immediate surroundings. Newspapers, magazines, and virtual communities all help students feel like they belong to something larger than their family or classroom. Virtual art experiences and field trips help students to vicariously experience beauty and awe as it exists in the world far beyond the classroom. Even online interaction with significant people through interviews and archives can promote the use of the existential intelligence.

The one caveat that has to be made here is that applications are not so neatly categorized by intelligences. Even though an HTML editing program like DreamWeaver seems to be a visual tool at first glance, consider the intra- and interpersonal dynamics that come into play as a Web site is formed. Or then again, the use of a listening center might be construed as a verbal/linguistic activity rather than as a musical/rhythmic task. In fact, it is both. My point is this: the only way to determine the intelligences a technology stimulates is to look at the task the technology is being used to accomplish. The technology itself is not a goal for instruction; it is merely a tool to help you accomplish that goal. It is in the process of instruction identified by a learning objective that we see the true nature of any technology and its relationship to the intelligences.

Criteria for Instructional Media

Dr. Sheryl Asen has identified 10 criteria to apply when incorporating technology into instruction. By measuring the use of a technology against these criteria, we can determine how educationally sound it is for instruction.

1. Students are involved in tasks that are broad in scope and challenging. Activities should span a range of experiences and be intellectually demanding. (Existential)

2. Students rather than the teacher have control over the learning process. The teacher serves more as a guide and coach than as a supervisor or administrator. (Intrapersonal)

3. Students work collaboratively and cooperatively. Learning tasks should not be completed in isolation. (Interpersonal, Kinesthetic)

4. Students practice and apply communication skills during learning. Learning tasks should promote discussion and interaction. (Verbal/Linguistic)

5. Students participate in varied learning tasks. This includes both variations in the format of the activities and in their objectives. (Musical/Rhythmic, Kinesthetic)

6. Students have opportunities to address learning tasks in different ways. In this way different approaches to a presented activity can be explored. (Naturalist)

7. Students apply higher order thinking skills through problem-solving tasks. Activities do more than ask students to recall rote facts, terms, and definitions. (Logical/Mathematical)

8. Students are encouraged to offer varied solutions to a given problem. Standard responses are not the only ones accepted; other answers can be acknowledged as acceptable. (Visual/Spatial)

9. Students are encouraged to contribute personal ideas and experiences to the learning task. There is validation of student input into the learning process. (Intrapersonal)

10. Students are intrinsically motivated by the prescribed learning tasks. Accomplishing the task is rewarding on its own merits regardless of the technologies being used. (Existential)

(From "Guidelines for Selecting or Creating Technology Assisted Learning Experiences" in *Teaching and Learning with Technology* by Sheryl Asen, copyright 1992. Used with permission.)

Note how well Asen's criteria match with Gardner's intelligences. From the objective to the assessment and at every step in between, MI theory can help teachers expand their repertoire of instructional strategies and balance their selection of resources and materials.

Let's return to the process we discussed at the beginning of this chapter. To properly select a medium for instruction, we need to properly identify the instructional context. To do so we must identify these four aspects of a lesson.

Teachers often take the first step—identifying the learner—for granted. It's so tempting to assume that one size fits all; by aiming for the middle of the class's ability range everyone will approximately master the lesson to some degree. Why not? That was the ideal of the Industrial Age.

But if we truly look at the distribution of intelligences in the classroom it quickly becomes apparent that one size does not fit all. Everyone is capable in his or her own way! Second, you must know your learning objective and the observable behaviors you want your learners to demonstrate. The activities you select for the lesson should match the learner to the objective. Once you have accomplished this, you can easily identify the intelligences you want to target for the lesson and the most appropriate technology or technologies.

For example, Ms. Donohue is preparing to teach her annual lesson on finding the mean, median, and mode in statistical analysis of data. In considering her learners, she keeps in mind the MI survey she administered at the beginning of the year. This is predominantly a group of visual learners, and they won't pick up on these abstract mathematical concepts quickly through rote drill and practice. Ms. Donohue considers the intelligences she wants to stimulate in this lesson and identifies the visual, naturalist, and interpersonal as the three to emphasize. After much consideration, she comes up with a lesson that uses spreadsheets and their associated graphing capabilities to introduce these concepts. The lesson plan is shown in Table 6. (Table 6 appears at the end of this chapter.)

Proper media selection is a must if MI and technology are to be applied effectively in instruction. Note how the objectives and materials correspond to the visual and naturalist intelligences in the given example. Of course, the procedure will dictate the interpersonal quality of the lesson. Ms. Donohue's lesson planning is off to a great start.

Reflections

1 Do you agree that the objective and the learner need to be considered before the intelligences and technologies? Why or why not?

2 How can ineffective media selection interfere with accommodation of the intelligences in instruction?

3 Conduct a learning materials inventory in your building. Which intelligences are best supported by the technologies you own?

Table 6

"Mean, Median, and Mode" Lesson

LESSON TITLE: Mean, Median, and Mode		TEACHER: Donohue	
GRADE LEVEL: 4			
SUBJECT(S): Math DATE: February 7, 2002		TIME: 10:15–11:05	

OBJECTIVE(S):	INTELLIGENCES:	TECHNOLOGIES:	NETS FOR STUDENTS:
1. Given a set of data and a spreadsheet, learners will work in pairs to create formulae that will identify the mean, median, and mode.	Naturalist Interpersonal	Spreadsheet	3. Students use technology tools to enhance learning, increase productivity, and promote creativity.
2. Given a set of data with identified mean, median, and mode, each pair of learners will create and print a table and graph that represent their findings.	Visual Interpersonal	Spreadsheet	

MATERIALS:	INTELLIGENCES:
Hard copies of sets of data	Visual
Spreadsheet	Naturalist

Chapter 5

Software Selection

The software market has grown exponentially in the last 20 years as the demand for a wide range of applications has increased. Educational software in particular has become a viable market as educators and parents alike have sought titles that meet the learning needs of children. Because market forces dictate so much of what is published, it is much easier to locate titles by content area and high-interest topic than it is to identify titles by the different intelligences children use to learn.

Categories of Software

To begin the process, consider these categories of software:

TUTORIAL—offers content, concepts, and skills with the opportunity for their application

GUIDED PRACTICE—teaches application of specific skills with support, interaction, and feedback

INDEPENDENT PRACTICE—uses a specific skill to reach an identified goal

ASSESSMENT—evaluates student mastery of specified skills and concepts through appropriate tasks

HEURISTIC—requires problem-solving skills that provide more than one strategy to successfully complete the tasks

PRODUCTIVITY—uses writing, composing, organizing, sorting, calculating, drawing, painting, and publishing

SIMULATION—provides a vicarious experience for students through electronic means

Software and Intelligences

There are many different kinds of software available to educators. Knowing the categories of software can help you assess the strengths and weaknesses of your software library. Looking at software by the intelligences they stimulate can further reveal which paths to learning you already support through software. Table 7 categorizes software both by Gardner's intelligences and Bloom's taxonomy.

From 1948 through 1956, Benjamin Bloom of the University of Chicago headed up a group of educational psychologists who constructed a hierarchy of the cognitive domain of learning. The framework consisted of six levels ranging from lower level thinking skills to the higher levels of human cognition. The resulting work became known as Bloom's Taxonomy. To appreciate the impact of this work, you may wish

Table 7

Software by Intelligence and Level of Thinking

SOFTWARE CATEGORY	INTELLIGENCES	BLOOM
TUTORIAL	Logical Verbal	Knowledge Comprehension
ASSESSMENT	Logical Verbal	Knowledge Comprehension
GUIDED PRACTICE	Logical Verbal Musical Naturalist	Knowledge Comprehension Application
INDEPENDENT PRACTICE	Logical Verbal Musical Naturalist Intrapersonal	Knowledge Comprehension Application Analysis
HEURISTIC	Logical Verbal Musical Naturalist Intrapersonal Interpersonal	Knowledge Comprehension Application Analysis Synthesis
SIMULATION	Logical Verbal Musical Naturalist Intrapersonal Interpersonal Visual Existential Kinesthetic	Knowledge Comprehension Application Analysis Synthesis
PRODUCTIVITY	Logical Verbal Musical Naturalist Intrapersonal Interpersonal Visual Existential Kinesthetic	Knowledge Comprehension Application Analysis Synthesis Evaluation

to read Bloom's *Taxonomy of Educational Objectives: The Classification of Educational Goals.*

Certainly, software can be designed to address more intelligences or higher levels of thinking than those identified in Table 7, but in isolation these are the minimum attributes for each software category.

Consider the implications of breaking down software in this way:

■ **TUTORIAL AND ASSESSMENT APPLICATIONS.** These address at least the logical and verbal intelligences at the lowest levels of Bloom's taxonomy. Can't these applications involve visuals, auditory effects, and other extras? Of course. But look at the process these applications take the learner through to accomplish a task. They tend to be very linear and depend on a learner's ability to recall, restate, or identify.

■ **GUIDED AND INDEPENDENT PRACTICE APPLICATIONS.** These bring in the musical and naturalist intelligences as students are invited to find and apply patterns and make sense of content in different contexts. This involves the levels of application in guided practice and application and analysis in the independent practice phase.

■ **HEURISTIC AND SIMULATION SOFTWARE.** These add the emotional intelligences—interpersonal and intrapersonal. In problem solving, this allows for the use of individual values and attitudes and the opportunity to participate in group collaboration. In simulations, students can also be engaged through the visual and existential intelligences as they place themselves in a virtual environment and apply their knowledge and skills to successfully complete tasks. Both heuristic and simulation applications promote the synthesis level in Bloom's taxonomy as students generate possible solutions to identified challenges.

■ **PRODUCTIVITY SOFTWARE.** This includes all the intelligences, including the kinesthetic, as students manipulate various tools to create their own original products. When students respond to one another's work, it stimulates the existential intelligence as well as the evaluation level in Bloom's taxonomy. Productivity applications can be the most useful in accommodating all the intelligences in your classroom.

Of course, the identified intelligences stimulated by any software depend on the context in which an application is used. A tutorial application can be used to stimulate a number of intelligences if it is used in consort with other instructional tasks. Likewise, a productivity tool such as a word processor can be used to stimulate the verbal intelligence by showing student understanding of vocabulary words at the knowledge level in Bloom's taxonomy. Context is the defining standard in applying Gardner's work. The categories I have suggested here are most useful in general terms and can be modified depending on your particular instructional technology practices.

On the other hand, there is a temptation to be all-inclusive in matching teaching materials to the intelligences. If you sit there and think about it long enough, any strategy or application can accommodate any intelligence with enough contortions and forced connections. But remember, Gardner's theory describes these pathways to learning in their natural state as they actually function in human cognition. The connections we make to the intelligences should be just as natural and logical as Gardner's; they should not be forced or contrived. To force unnatural connections is to sell your students short, for they won't be able to make the connections you intend and you'll have to revisit the entire skill or concept. If you're going to force connections to the intelligences so that you can claim your instruction is all-inclusive, you're only making an effort to justify the way you've always taught. Why bother? Once you start down the road of integrating MI into instruction, you make an implicit commitment to yourself to be honest, to be open to new possibilities, and to be willing to change.

Conducting an MI Software Inventory

The best way to know what software you have and how it can be used is to take a software inventory. Get a master list of software library titles and plug them into a table that categorizes each application by the intelligences it addresses. Table 8 provides a brief example of a software inventory.

Table 8

Software Inventory

	VERB	LOGIC	VISU	KINES	MUSIC	INTRA	INTER	NATUR	EXIST
ACCEL READER	✓	✓							
KIDPIX	✓		✓	✓	✓	✓			✓
TIMELINER		✓	✓		✓			✓	
OREGON TRAIL		✓	✓	✓	✓	✓	✓	✓	✓

It is important to check off only those intelligences that are primarily stimulated by each application's affordances. Accelerated Reader, for example, primarily stimulates the verbal and logical intelligences through its emphasis on reading comprehension and its multiple-choice quiz format. Timeliner, on the other hand, stimulates the logical and visual intelligences through its timeline features, the musical intelligence through the patterns one can pick up by interacting with a timeline, and the naturalist intelligence through the different kinds of categories and hierarchies one can create using this software. Certainly KidPix could have a logical or interpersonal component to it if the lesson is designed to accommodate those specific intelligences, but that isn't what you're evaluating in this inventory. The point is to determine the intelligences each application supports on its own merits before instruction takes place. In completing an MI software inventory, you can also identify those intelligences that need to be considered in future software purchases.

Another way to evaluate software is through its content, interface, design, and documentation features. Here are some essential questions to ask when taking this approach. (An MI Software Evaluation Rubric is on the CD-ROM in the MI_Evaluation_Tools file.)

Design

- Is the software interactive and responsive to student input?

  Do intelligences become activated through the input and responses students exchange with the application?

- Does the design provide for a variety of intelligences?

  Are there multiple ways to successfully accomplish tasks in the application, or must everyone use the same strategies and orientation?

- Is there evidence of scaffolding to support learners as they strengthen less developed intelligences?

  Does the application provide support for students who may not feel as confident or comfortable completing certain kinds of tasks because of their personal distribution of intelligences?

- Are there ways to extend the learning experience from the software into the classroom?

  Can you adapt the application's instructional strategies into classroom lessons that will reinforce what students are practicing?

- If assessment takes place, does it match the intelligences used in instruction?

  If there is testing or record keeping of skill mastery, does it provide assessment tasks that use the same intelligences targeted in the instructional tasks the application provides?

Content

- Do the software's objectives go beyond the lower levels of Bloom's taxonomy?

  Is the objective concerned with just skill, drill, and recall; or are students challenged to use the material in new and different ways to practice mastery?

- Does the content addressed in the software lend itself to uses across the curriculum?

  For example, does a mathematics application solely address an isolated math skill or does it have applications in other areas of your curriculum?

- Does the content lend itself to the perspective of several different intelligences?

  Is it strictly a linear, logical application; or can visual and existential learners appreciate its content too?

- Is the content adaptive to different intelligences, even those not addressed in the software itself?

    What are the possibilities for extending the content and skills in the application into other classroom activities?

- Do explanations, definitions, and directions accommodate different intelligences?

    Is there more than one way to learn in the application, or will it be optimal only for verbal or logical learners?

Interface

- Does the software intuitively adapt to the strengths of different intelligences?

    Can the application make adjustments based on the kinds of input it receives from students, or does it simply track ability level?

- Are there visual, auditory, and kinesthetic components to the software?

    Will students be able to navigate with ease through a variety of different kinds of prompts, or do the prompts tend to be strictly visual?

- Do the support and help functions accommodate students with different intelligences?

    When students look for assistance within the application itself, is it always verbal or logical or are there examples for kinesthetic and naturalist learners too?

- Do the metaphors used to explain software functions address varied intelligences?

    Are there only icons and buttons, or are other familiar contexts used, such as storybooks, playgrounds, neighborhoods, and families?

- Is navigation throughout the software global and open ended rather than linear and skill based?

    Do students have lots of choices, and can they make them without hindrance in any order they choose?

Documentation

- Do the manual and teacher support materials address different intelligences?

    Is there explicit treatment of different student orientations to learning in the support materials that come with the application?

- Do the manual and teacher support materials acknowledge higher order thinking skills?

    Are synthesis and evaluation tasks included at the higher end of the application's learning activities?

- Are extension activities included that can help address additional intelligences beyond the limitations of the software?

    Does the documentation include lesson plans or activity sheets that can help you transfer digital experiences into classroom activities?

- Are there recommended resources you can use to further enrich and extend the use of the software across the intelligences?

    Do the resources include online activities, print materials, and even additional software titles?

- Are there suggestions for alternative assessment tasks?

    If the application tends to provide verbal and logical assessment tasks, does the documentation also suggest other ways to assess student learning?

Of course, many software companies have not yet addressed the distribution of intelligences across a student population, so you probably will not see specific references to intelligences per se. But with your own MI awareness, you can identify the elements of well-designed software that accommodate MI no matter how the publisher packages it.

You will often want to know which software titles have already been classroom tested and are the popular choice of teachers around the country for instructional use. Table 9 provides a listing of software applications by intelligence that have been rated the best by educators from around North America.

The PEP Model

Regardless of the titles you select for instruction, the proof comes in the way they are used in instruction. A software application should not be an end unto itself. It should be part of a larger instructional approach that will help address a variety of intelligences in your classroom. This means you will want to set up the context for using the software prior to introducing it to students and provide follow-up activities that extend and enrich the learning experiences it provides. This practice of offering presoftware activities, followed by learning experiences with the software, and ending with postsoftware experiences that allow for accommodation of MI will be referred to here as the Presoftware, Experience, Postsoftware (PEP) model. This model can come in many shapes and sizes, but the intent is always the same: to infuse the technology into your instruction so thoroughly that it becomes a vital piece in the learning process.

Consider the software Accelerated Reader. It's quite easy to have the software in place, to tell your students to read books and take quizzes, and to rely on the software to keep track of each student's performance. But that leaves the use of Accelerated Reader as an extraneous task in your classroom because it exists on its own without any true tie-in to the meaningful learning you want to provide for your students each day. However, placing Accelerated Reader in the PEP model suddenly provides all kinds of connections to your curriculum.

Table 9

Software Application by Intelligence

APPLICATION	PURCHASING INFORMATION
BODILY/KINESTHETIC	
CyberStretch	www.cyberstretch.com/
IntelliTools	www.intellitools.com/
Lego Dacta	www.pitsco-legodacta.com/
Mavis Beacon	www.learningco.com/product.asp?OID=4142742&SC=1105647&CID=249
Probeware	www.teamlabs.com/
EXISTENTIAL	
ArtSpace	www.mprojects.wiu.edu/artspace.shtml
Geodesy	www.bgrg.com/geodesy/
Neighborhood Map Machine	www.tomsnyder.com/products/productdetail.asp?PS=NEINEI
SimCity	http://simcity.ea.com/us/guide/
Trudy's Time and Place House	www.edmark.com/prod/house/trudy/
With Open Eyes	www.artic.edu/aic/books/subwith.html
INTERPERSONAL	
CUseeMe	www1.fvc.com/products/cuseeme5.htm
Dreamweaver	www.macromedia.com/software/dreamweaver/
ICQ	http://web.icq.com/
Instant Messenger	http://aim.aol.com/
MMPI	www.psychscreen.com/p310.htm
Net Meeting	www.microsoft.com/windows/netmeeting/
INTRAPERSONAL	
Choices, Choices	www.tomsnyder.com/products/productdetail.asp?PS=CHOCHO
Decisions, Decisions	www.tomsnyder.com/products/productdetail.asp?PS=DECDEC
Feelings	www.cdgarden.com/main/software/mw/feelings.htm
Forrest Center Stage	www.orcca.com/MMProd.htm#Forrest
Perseus	www.perseus.com/
LOGICAL/MATHEMATICAL	
Graph Club	www.tomsnyder.com/products/productdetail.asp?PS=GRPGRT
Microsoft Excel	www.microsoft.com/office/excel/default.htm
MicroWorld	www.kidsandcomputers.com/
Millie's Math House	www.edmark.com/prod/house/millie/
Pre-Algebra World, Algebra World, Geometry World	www.cogtech.com/
Prime Time Math	www.sheppardsoftware.com/pmath1.htm
StageCast	www.tagdev.co.uk/products/stagecast/gen_stagecast.htm

Thanks to the members of the Tech Coordinators list (tlandeck@santacruz.k12.ca.us), the National Association for the Education of Young Children's list (LISTSERV@LISTSERV.UIUC.EDU), the Early Childhood Educator's list (www.ume.maine.edu/~cofed/eceol/), and the Connected Teacher mailing list (http://connectedteacher.classroom.com/listServ/subscribe.asp), all of whom submitted titles in consideration for inclusion in this listing.

TABLE 9 ■ SOFTWARE APPLICATION BY INTELLIGENCE

APPLICATION	PURCHASING INFORMATION
MUSICAL/RHYTHMIC	
Cubase	www.steinberg.net/products/ps/cubase/mac/vst/
Finale	www.codamusic.com/coda/
Introduction to Patterns	http://sunburst-store.com/cgi-bin/sunburst.storefront/ 3b35f5150adc6cc42717d00b893206cf/Product/View/8239&2D02
Music Ace	www.harmonicvision.com/products.htm
Sibelius	www.sibelius.com/
Thinkin' Things	www.edmark.com/prod/tt/
NATURALIST	
Amazing Animals	http://usstore.dk.com/shop/shared/product.asp?ISBN=0789433265
Chime Pro and ChemScape	www.mdli.com/cgi/dynamic/product.html?uid=$uid&key=$key&id=6
Field Trip to the Rainforest Deluxe	http://sunburst-store.com/cgi-bin/sunburst.storefront/ 3b35fc570ae863b02717d00b893206b3/Product/View/8319
FileMaker Pro	www.filemaker.com/products/compare_fm5.html
IHMC Concept Map Software	http://cmap.coginst.uwf.edu/
Inspiration/Kidspiration	www.inspiration.com/
Sammy's Science House	www.edmark.com/prod/house/sammy/
Stella	www.hps-inc.com/Education/new_Stella.htm
TimeLiner	www.tomsnyder.com/products/productdetail.asp?PS=TIMV50
VERBAL/LINGUISTIC	
AppleWorks	www.apple.com/appleworks/
Bailey's Book House	www.edmark.com/prod/house/bailey/
Clicker4	www.cricksoftware.com/clicker4/c4write.htm
Co:Writer	www.donjohnston.com/catalog/cow4000s.htm
Write:Out Loud	www.donjohnston.com/catalog/wols.htm
Microsoft Publisher	www.microsoft.com/office/publisher/default.htm
Microsoft Word	www.microsoft.com/office/word/default.htm
VISUAL/SPATIAL	
Flash	www.macromedia.com/software/flash/
Golly Gee Blocks	www.gollygee.com/
GraphMaster	www.tomsnyder.com/products/productdetail.asp?PS=GRAMAS
Green Globs and Graphing Equations	http://sunburst-store.com/cgi-bin/sunburst.storefront/ 3b35f2d20ad5e0642717d00b893206ee/Product/View/9372
HyperStudio	www.hyperstudio.com/
iMovie	www.apple.com/imovie/
KidPix	www.kidpix.com/
Microsoft PowerPoint	www.microsoft.com/office/powerpoint/
NIH Image	http://rsb.info.nih.gov/nih-image/index.html
Adobe Photoshop	www.adobe.com/products/photoshop/
Tessellation Exploration	www.tomsnyder.com/products/productdetail.asp?ps=TESEXP

PRESOFTWARE: Each month, identify a genre for students to read. Discuss the characteristics of the genre and have your librarian put Accelerated Reader titles from this genre on loan to your students. Work with students to plan a culminating activity at the end of the month that will celebrate this genre. Perhaps the videotaping of booktalks or asking each student to dress as a character from a specific book in the genre would be appropriate. Students might even like to design their own Accelerated Reader quizzes for a book of their choice.

EXPERIENCE: Have students select titles from the classroom collection of the genre and complete Accelerated Reader quizzes as they finish reading each title. Continue studying the genre in class.

POSTSOFTWARE: Complete the culminating task you and the class agreed on at the beginning of the month. Pass out Accelerated Reader certificates indicating the points each student earned during the process. Review the genre and offer an extension activity in which groups of students work on writing their own stories in the genre's format.

In Table 10, notice how a decidedly verbal and logical software application becomes easily adaptable for a variety of intelligences simply because the teacher used the PEP model in the planning process. (The CD-ROM accompanying this book contains a blank PEP chart in the MI_Evaluation_Tools file.)

Table 10

Example of Planning Using PEP

PRESOFTWARE	EXPERIENCE	POSTSOFTWARE
Identify the genre	Read books in the genre	Design original AR quizzes
Identify cumulative activity	Complete AR quizzes	Pass out AR points

Table 11 provides an example of how one teacher, Ms. Mannas, sets up software applications within the context of a larger unit to provide rich, meaningful learning that will transfer across intelligences.

The two presentation days are scheduled with the classes involved, and parents are invited to view their children's work. (Verbal, Intrapersonal). A CD containing the class presentations is burned and used in the library as a reference source.

Integrating a software application into instruction can be so seamless a part of the process that students naturally use it in learning and demonstrating understanding. The PEP model can help you achieve this kind of second-nature technology use in the classroom.

Table 11

"Multimedia Presentation on Animal Dissection" Lesson

LESSON TITLE: Multimedia Presentation on Animal Dissection			TEACHER: Susan Mannas St. Theresa School
GRADE LEVEL: 5			Austin, Texas
SUBJECT(S): Science	DATE: September-October	TIME: 14 45-minute periods	

OBJECTIVE(S):	INTELLIGENCES:	TECHNOLOGIES:	NETS FOR STUDENTS:
All fifth-grade students will build and present a multimedia presentation comparing and contrasting the four animals they dissected in science class.	Verbal Musical Logical Naturalist Interpersonal Visual Intrapersonal	Computer, scanner, CD burner, HyperStudio, Internet Explorer, Word, Inspiration	5. Students use technology tools to process data and report results.

MATERIALS:	INTELLIGENCES:
Science binder with dissection information, Internet resources sheet, grading rubric	Verbal Visual Logical Musical Naturalist Intrapersonal

PROCEDURE:	INTELLIGENCES:
Prelesson: Students spent several months in science class participating in dissecting four animals—a worm, grasshopper, starfish, and squid. They took many notes as they learned about these animals. The science teacher and I created a rubric that cited the information to be included in the presentation. Students also spent time prior to this assignment learning how HyperStudio works. **Lesson:** **Day 1:** Go over rubric.	Visual Logical Verbal Naturalist

TABLE 11 ■ "MULTIMEDIA PRESENTATION ON ANIMAL DISSECTION" LESSON	
PROCEDURE:	**INTELLIGENCES:**
Days 2-4: Build skeleton pages, work on organization of stack and navigational buttons.	Visual Logical Verbal Naturalist
Day 4: Introduce Web sites from which graphics will be collected. Teach students how to cite their references under the image that they used and how to include it on their credits page.	Visual Verbal Logical
Day 5: Scan "squid ink" pictures. (When the students dissected the squid, some of the squid still had ink in them. The students were allowed to create pictures with this ink. We then scanned the pictures and placed them in a shared folder so they could include these pictures in their projects.)	Visual Naturalist
Days 2-10: Students build their stacks and include the topics from the rubric.	Verbal Musical Logical Naturalist Interpersonal Visual Intrapersonal
Day 11: Students are reminded to check their stacks to make sure they have included the areas on the rubric. They check their navigation and are allowed to add sound. (If students are allowed to add sound as they go, some won't get the "meat" of their project done. They will spend the whole time focusing on sound.)	Musical
Day 12: Finishing touches	Intrapersonal
Days 13-14: Presentations	Interpersonal Visual
ASSESSMENT:	**INTELLIGENCE:**
Grading rubric	Spatial Logical Verbal Visual Naturalist

Reflections

1 What would Susan Mannas's PEP chart look like for the Animal Dissection lesson presented in this chapter?

2 Take an inventory of your school's software library. Which categories of software does your collection emphasize? Which categories are not well represented? Which intelligences are best addressed by the titles in your software collection?

3 What titles would you add to the software listed in Table 9?

Chapter 6

Modifying Existing Lessons

One of the appealing features of Gardner's theory is that it confirms so much of the work teachers already do in the classroom. Good teachers have been instinctively catering to different intelligences without even knowing about the MI model. Presenting Gardner to teachers is a pleasure because his work validates so many good things they have already done. This makes for a sound marriage of theory and practice because teachers are immediately ready to take a look at their classroom-tested lessons and units and superimpose them on the MI model. It sounds easy enough, right? But you'd be surprised how working through this process raises as many questions as it does answers! In this chapter I offer for your consideration the POMAT (Procedure, Objective, Materials, Assessment, Technology) approach for existing lessons.

A Rationale for Modifying Lessons

For the last half-century, teachers have come to expect textbook publishers and curriculum marketers to put together prepackaged instructional programs that are a combination of salesmanship, structure, and resources. While many reform movements have bemoaned a situation in which the commercial tail is wagging the educational dog, teachers have, in fact, grown quite accustomed to having a prepackaged program in place that they can at least borrow from and refer to as needed. It's convenient and it saves time. Moreover, it's familiar after five decades; it's comfortable. Gardner, on the other hand, does not advocate the prepackaging of MI theory. MI is as unique as each individual learner, and it requires the blend of a teacher's personal instructional style with the combination of student MI profiles in the teacher's classroom. That's not to say we're not already beginning to see companies trying to package and sell an MI approach to instruction. If they can sell it, they'll market it! It simply means that it may not be appropriate for effective instruction.

Having said this up front, I know that teachers approach analyzing and revising existing lessons or units with good intentions and a certain amount of uncertainty. They need to ask several important question:

- Will I have to revise my objectives?

- How do I decide which intelligences to employ?

- Should I incorporate all the intelligences into a lesson?

The answers are not at all clear-cut and obvious once you start looking at your own work.

First, let's state the reason for modifying existing lessons: teachers should edit and revise existing lessons and units in order to maximize the accommodation of intelligences in their instruction. This should not be an exercise in documenting the intelligences your lessons and units already address. To simply label existing lessons by the intelligences they accommodate is to spend time you don't have validating lessons you don't intend to change. The only commonsense rationale for this exercise is to take lessons you already know and love and improve them by making additional connections for all of your students.

Also, we should have a working definition of what it means to accommodate, stimulate, or otherwise employ an intelligence in a lesson. Exercising an intelligence by definition means that an activity is in place that uses that intelligence for the explicit purpose of instruction. For example, the fact that students talk with one another while completing a lab experiment is not an exercise of the verbal intelligence. Talking while working is not in and of itself supportive of the instructional outcome. On the other hand, having students brainstorm together for possible solutions as part of a creative problem-solving activity builds toward the outcome of the lesson. It is by definition an accommodation of the verbal intelligence. Another example is Gardner's humorous anecdote about being welcomed into a kindergarten classroom where he observed children crawling on their hands and knees, yelping and howling. After asking the teacher about the activity, Gardner was informed that the children were exercising their kinesthetic intelligence. Unimpressed, Gardner responded that this was not kinesthetic intelligence but merely a group of children crawling on the floor and howling like wolves! Keep this story in mind as you identify intelligences in existing lessons.

After you have a clear rationale for modifying lessons and units, you need to be assured that no one lesson will accommodate all the intelligences. Forcing all nine intelligences into one finite lesson would be so contrived that students would not benefit from the resulting saturation of experiences the lesson would attempt to provide. As we walk through this process, expect to integrate possibly three to five intelligences into one lesson. These intelligences will become evident as you examine an existing lesson because they will naturally flow from the content of your plan. This is important because children need to see natural, obvious connections of the intelligences if they are going to truly benefit from your efforts. If your lesson tries to force an intrapersonal connection that just doesn't make sense in the flow of the rest of the lesson, it will tend to throw your students off the objective rather than help them understand it. In short, if the introduction of an intelligence into an existing lesson doesn't fit quickly and easily into your plan, omit it. When in doubt, leave it out!

As for the proper design of an MI lesson, the objective must first be in place. Continually look back to the stated objective to make sure that you remain on course for the intended learning that is to take place. For an existing lesson, this may mean modifying the objective from its current form or simply acknowledging the objective as is. With the objective in place, you can then look to the intelligences you want to include in your lesson. There should be an obvious, natural connection between any intelligence you identify and your objective. Intelligences should reflect the goals of your lesson and flow from the actions stated in the objective of your lesson. Finally, with the objective and intelligences identified, you can then decide on the technologies, if any, that you would like to use in the lesson. Not every lesson will benefit from the use of technology, and knowing when it is appropriate to use a technology comes with practice and experience. As you start the process of modifying lessons, your purpose is to help students reach your stated objective by incorporating technologies that stimulate the intelligences.

The POMAT Method

The rote practice of declaring the objective, intelligences, and technologies you intend to use in a lesson can quickly be reduced to going through the motions without using a critical eye. From my own personal experience I can attest to the fact that after a few lessons it's easy to fall into a pattern of using similar sounding objectives with familiar intelligences and favorite technology applications. People are, after all, creatures of habit, and it's hard to look at every new lesson with a fresh eye. For this reason I have developed the POMAT (Procedure, Objective, Materials, Assessment, Technology) approach to modifying existing lessons for MI and technology. The POMAT process breaks up the lesson revision process into five steps that require you to think about how well your lesson maps itself.

The POMAT approach is built on the notion of backward planning, developed by Wiggins and McTighe, from the view of the teacher-practitioner. The teacher first looks at the procedure of a lesson and then maps back through the objective, materials, and assessment to determine a consistency of purpose. If the actual flow of a lesson nicely matches the objective and assessment, it is of sound design and will bring maximum instructional success. If a lesson is inconsistent in each of its critical components, the POMAT process will identify gaps and weaknesses that the teacher can then address. The entire procedure is designed to examine a lesson's consistency within the context of the nine intelligences. Here are the five steps of POMAT:

1. **PROCEDURE**—Without looking at any other part of the existing lesson, go directly to the procedure and make notes on each prescribed activity and what intelligences it accommodates. For example, if students are asked to select a type of bridge from a previous lesson to employ in their design, you could note the naturalist intelligence (the intelligence of categories and hierarchies) on the POMAT chart (see Table 12). If students are then asked to calculate the dimensions of a bridge they are to build, you might note on the POMAT chart that this stimulates the logical intelligence. Complete this process for the entire lesson's procedure, noting any and all intelligences that are accommodated.

2. **OBJECTIVE**—Now go back to the beginning of your lesson plan and examine your stated objective. Note on the POMAT chart which intelligences the objective suggests will be accommodated. For instance, if the objective states that the learner will construct a bridge 3 feet long that will allow a 12-pound remote-control truck to cross safely 2 feet off the floor, you may note that it accommodates the logical and kinesthetic intelligences. Be sure to note only the intelligences the objective clearly accommodates.

3. **MATERIALS**—With the procedure and objective reviewed, you can now look at the list of materials you have generated for the lesson. Which intelligences do these materials stimulate? Note that the building supplies and hand tools accommodate the logical, visual, and kinesthetic intelligences in the POMAT chart.

4. **ASSESSMENT**—Now you can look at your stated form of assessment for the lesson. Is it consistent with the procedure, objective, and materials in the intelligences it utilizes? Is there a clear connection between the objective, materials, procedure, and assessment task? In the case of the lesson on bridge construction, testing the bridge with the 12-pound truck rolling over it is the test of choice. It is practical, verifiable, and something that will create an exciting culminating event for the class. If your assessment matches well with your objective and the intelligences you have identified throughout the lesson, you're on solid ground!

5. **TECHNOLOGY**—Finally, you can examine your lesson through the POMAT chart and determine which technologies, if any, should be included. You are probably already employing certain industrial technologies in the lesson. But what about digital technologies? Is this a good activity for introducing Probeware? If you project a spreadsheet on the wall and fill in the data for each bridge the class has constructed, will that be an appropriate use of technology? Or maybe the digital camera could be used to take pictures of the students at work so that the class can work on a multimedia presentation of their experiences. Then again, what if you plan ahead for next year, invite classes to participate online in a competition to build an effective bridge that meets the lesson objective, and compare your class results against the data from other classes? How do you know which is the most effective use of technology?

The CD-ROM accompanying this book contains a blank POMAT chart in the MI_Evaluation_Tools file. Table 12 shows the five POMAT steps in a culminating lesson for a unit on bridges.

A visual scan of the POMAT chart quickly identifies areas of strength in your lesson. The bridge construction task is a strongly logical, problem-solving task with visual and kinesthetic implications for the learner. There's an interpersonal dimension to the task, and students conduct organizing and categorizing activities as they go. You probably already knew this from your past experiences in implementing this lesson. But look where the lesson comes up empty! For all the chatter that fills your room as students purposefully work, there's no direct link between the lesson objective and the verbal intelligence. Also, for as many patterns as bridges create, and for as much aesthetic beauty as they can add to the environment, neither the musical nor the existential intelligences have instructional connections here. Picture a child in your class who is very verbal but has a hard time generating effective solutions to problems, or a student who has strong personal convictions and is thus preoccupied with the impact of bridges on the surrounding landscape. As creative and hands-on as your lesson is, it misses the opportunity to connect with these students.

Table 12

The POMAT Chart

POMAT	VL	ML	VS	BK	MR	IE	IA	NT	EX	NOTES
PROCEDURE		✓	✓	✓		✓		✓		Organizing, building, measuring, problem solving, working in groups
OBJECTIVE		✓		✓						Problem solving and building
MATERIALS		✓	✓	✓						Hand tools, rulers, balsa wood, nails, screws, safety goggles, information books, paper, pencil
ASSESSMENT		✓					✓	✓		Driving 10 pound remote control truck over bridge, identifying the best bridge designs
TECHNOLOGY		✓	✓	✓						Hand tools, rulers, nails, screws, remote control truck

VL=VERBAL/LINGUISTIC	**ML=MATHEMATICAL/LOGICAL**	**VS=VISUAL/SPATIAL**
BK=BODILY/KINESTHETIC	**MR=MUSICAL**	**IE=INTERPERSONAL**
IA=INTRAPERSONAL	**NT=NATURALIST**	**EX=EXISTENTIAL**

From this summary of the POMAT exercise, which digital application might be most appropriate to incorporate into this lesson: Probeware, Excel, PowerPoint, or an online collaborative project? Let's see what we know already. Probeware is a wonderful application that allows students to see digital representations of their experiments. It clearly has both visual/spatial and mathematical/logical applications, which are two intelligences the task already targets. If you wish to bolster the visual/spatial component of this lesson, then Probeware would be a good choice. Excel is great for stimulating the mathematical/logical and naturalist intelligences with the possibility of making connections to the visual intelligence via a graph or chart. If you would like to reinforce the visual/spatial and mathematical/logical intelligences and beef up the naturalist intelligence in the lesson, Excel is clearly your choice. PowerPoint is a multimedia presentation tool that, in combination with a digital camera, would make excellent use of the verbal, visual, and interpersonal intelligences. It also includes a nonlinear component that may be used by learners who want to see many relationships among ideas. Finally, an online collaborative project would reinforce the emphasis on the logical, visual, and kinesthetic intelligences while adding to the inter- and intrapersonal components, as well as the possibility of accommodating the musical and existential intelligences. In summary, there's no one right answer—you need to determine the most effective focus for your lesson!

Look at how much more clearly you can see your choices now. No, it's not prepackaged and ready to fly, and there's no one right answer. You have to fill in the context for the lesson to determine the answer that's right for you. You can decide to:

- not use digital technologies so that the lesson is kept finite and intact.

- add nontechnological tasks (oral presentations, identification of patterns in bridge design, discussion of bridge aesthetics and its impact on the environment) to the lesson to stimulate additional intelligences.

- use Probeware or Excel to enhance the lesson objective.

- use PowerPoint to extend the lesson without changing its primary focus.

- choose the online collaborative project and develop a unit that will take the lesson in a completely new direction that opens it up for all the intelligences.

The choice is yours!

Some Practical Examples

In addition to mapping out a lesson in POMAT, you can examine the balance of intelligences in your plan by using the Wheel of MI Domains (see Chapter 2) to ensure that you cover all three MI domains and help all students make connections in your lesson. Consider Mrs. Betteridge's favorite kindergarten lesson on sinking and floating. For years she has done a lesson with a large tub of water and all kinds of materials children can experiment with. She is wondering how her lesson fares in stimulating her students' intelligences. Mrs. Betteridge considers her objectives for the lesson.

Objectives

1. The learner will predict with at least 75% success whether a given material will sink or float.

2. The learner will sort the materials into two groups: sinking and floating.

Mrs. Betteridge looks at the MI wheel and quickly identifies Objective 1 as addressing the logical intelligence. After much thought she decides that Objective 2 addresses both the musical and naturalist intelligences. In short, she has a highly analytic lesson. Is there anything wrong with having a highly analytic lesson? No, not at all! However, Mrs. Betteridge is looking to expand the scope of this lesson to stimulate additional intelligences in her classroom, so she returns to the MI wheel to consider the best ways to further integrate intelligences into her lesson. After further consideration, Mrs. Betteridge determines that, while there is a strong kinesthetic component to the activity, she would like to bolster it a little more by having the students weigh each material before testing their hypothesis. In this way they can use the information in forming their hypothesis, and they can sort materials not only by sinking and floating but also by weight. Also, she wants the children to use their visual intelligence by using drawings of each material to create a diagram that shows their findings. As a result of this process, her objectives now look like this:

Objectives

1 The learner will weigh with at least 80% accuracy each material in both a dry and wet state. (Kinesthetic, Logical)

2. The learner will predict with at least 75% success whether a given material will sink or float. (Musical, Logical)

3. The learner will sort the materials into four groups: sinking, floating, dry weight, and wet weight. (Naturalist)

4. Using picture symbols, the learner will create a diagram that reflects the information he or she has gathered from the experiment. (Visual)

Now Mrs. Betteridge is ready to tighten up her lesson and successfully address five of the nine intelligences. Used this way the MI wheel can be an extremely useful tool for balancing existing lessons beyond the POMAT chart.

Table 13 shows how Leigh Anne Rogers made her second-grade dinosaur unit come alive by considering MI theory and the uses of technology. Table 14 shows how Leigh Anne's unit looks in a POMAT chart. (Tables 13 and 14 appear at the end of this chapter.)

Note how explicitly Leigh Anne hits all nine intelligences throughout the course of her unit. Her objectives, materials, and assessments follow nicely through on this, stimulating all but the intrapersonal and existential intelligences. The technologies employed address six of the nine intelligences in her students. Leigh Anne may seek to find ways to incorporate the interpersonal intelligence in her selection of technologies, but this is a well-distributed accommodation of the intelligences!

Reflections

❶ Can intelligences affect your instructional approach much as they affect student approaches to learning?

❷ Which intelligences are easiest for you to accommodate in your classroom? Why?

❸ Which technologies do you use most frequently? Which intelligences do they best accommodate?

❹ How can the POMAT approach help you maximize the potential of existing lessons for MI and technology?

Table 13

"Integrated Dinosaur Research" Unit

UNIT TITLE: Integrated Dinosaur Research		TEACHER: Leigh Ann Rogers Indian Creek Elementary School Olathe, Kansas	
GRADE LEVEL: 2			
SUBJECT(S): Arts, Language Arts, Math, Science		TIME FRAME: 10 days (2 weeks)	
OBJECTIVE (S):	**INTELLIGENCES:**	**TECHNOLOGIES:**	**NETS FOR STUDENTS:**
Art 1. Make connections between visual art and language arts, math, and science.	Naturalist, Existential	Computer, VCR, projector/monitor, Inspiration	6. Technology problem-solving and decision-making tools: Students employ technology in the development of strategies for solving problems in the real world.
Language Arts 1. Before reading: make predictions, generate prior knowledge, preview text and text structure, formulate questions, set a purpose for reading 2. During reading: confirm, reject, generate predictions, answer prereading questions, expand prior knowledge, summarize 3. After reading: identify, tell or write the main idea/ details, sequence events, link causes to effects, create graphic organizers 4. Information and study skills: use parts of a book to locate information, use charts, graphs, tables, and maps	Verbal Visual Logical Musical Interpersonal Naturalist	Computer, VCR, projector/monitor, references, Inspiration, Excel, Internet Explorer	5. Technology research tools: Students evaluate and select new information resources and technological innovations based on the appropriateness for specific tasks. 6. Technology problem-solving and decision-making tools: Students use technology resources for solving problems and making

TABLE 13 ■ "INTEGRATED DINOSAUR RESEARCH" UNIT			
OBJECTIVE (S):	**INTELLIGENCES:**		**NETS FOR STUDENTS:**
5. Listening: demonstrate active listening 6. Speaking: demonstrate effective oral communication, organize and express thoughts in a logical sequence 7. Research: determine focus of research and identify information, seek information and identify best sources, locate sources and access information, select and use relevant information, organize and present information gathered			informed decisions.
Math 1. Read and write whole numbers to 1,000 2. Use measurement tools for volume, length, temperature, weight 3. Construct graphs, including title, axes, tables, number scales 4. Collect data	Verbal Visual Kinesthetic Naturalist	Computer, VCR, projector/monitor, measuring cup, measuring tape, scale, thermo-meter, Excel	5. Technology research tools: Students use technology tools to process data and report results.
Science 1. Learn to apply the inquiry process by classifying and ordering objects, collect and record data and make simple predictions 2. Explain that the earth is covered with many types of rocks and soil	Verbal Naturalist Existential	Computer, VCR, projector/monitor, Inspiration, Excel	5. Technology research tools: Students use technology to locate, evaluate. andcollect information.

TABLE 13 ■ "INTEGRATED DINOSAUR RESEARCH" UNIT	
MATERIALS:	**INTELLIGENCES:**
Literature:	Verbal
Various Encyclopedia sets, as available	Visual
Dinosaurs Are Different (Aliki)	Logical
Giant Dinosaurs (Erna Rowe)	Naturalist
Dinosaurs Walked Here (Patricia Lauber)	
Fossils (Alan Roberts)	
Digging for Dinosaurs (Cheryl Naus)	
Other dinosaur titles from library and personal collections brought in by students	
Bernard Most titles for Author Study: *If the Dinosaurs Came Back, Whatever Happened to the Dinosaurs, Dinosaur Cousins, The Littlest Dinosaurs*	
Various dinosaur-related poetry	Verbal Visual Musical
Videos:	Verbal
Eyewitness Dinosaur (Lionheart Television)	Visual
Death of the Dinosaur (Turner Home Entertainment)	Musical
Magic School Bus in the Time of the Dinosaurs (Joanna Cole)	

DAILY TASKS:
 	
Prelesson Class Preparation:
 	
  ■ Run materials for dinosaur sort (AIMS).
 	
  ■ Purchase gummy dinosaurs for sort.
 	
  ■ Gather materials.
 	
  ■ Contact Children's Museum of Kansas City to schedule a visit with the Classroom on Wheels. (This is a mobile classroom with a themed lesson on excavating fossils. It's like a field trip that visits you!)
 	
  ■ Search Internet and bookmark appropriate sites for student use.
 	
  ■ Schedule library research time.	

TABLE 13 ■ "INTEGRATED DINOSAUR RESEARCH" UNIT	
DAILY TASKS:	**INTELLIGENCES:**
■ Send notes home to parents about food needed for culminating activity. ■ Organize centers: listening center with dinosaur books, Internet on networked computer, art center to draw and color different dinosaurs, poetry center with dinosaur poetry, math center with measurement activities and graphing activities.	
Procedure:	
Day 1:	
■ Students complete web about dinosaurs in computer lab using Inspiration software, adding all of the information that they already know. ■ After returning to the classroom, an entire class web is made. Students also record any questions they may have. ■ Read *Giant Dinosaurs* together and complete comprehension activity. Measure some of the actual giant lengths within the school building.	Verbal Logical Visual Naturalist Existentialist
Day 2:	
■ Explore Web sites as a class. Sites are then made available as a center choice. ■ In small groups, students read various Bernard Most titles and work together on comprehension activities.	Verbal Logical Visual Intrapersonal Interpersonal Existentialist
Day 3:	
■ Small groups continue to read various Bernard Most titles. ■ Teacher reads *If the Dinosaurs Came Back* aloud. Students create a classroom mural following the artist's style in the book illustrations.	Verbal Visual Kinesthetic Intrapersonal Interpersonal Existentialist
Day 4:	
■ Read *Digging for Dinosaurs* aloud as a class. Explore fossil collections from teacher and students who brought them to share.	Verbal Logical Visual Interpersonal Naturalist

TABLE 13 ■ "INTEGRATED DINOSAUR RESEARCH" UNIT	
DAILY TASKS:	**INTELLIGENCES:**
Day 5:	
■ Visit Classroom on Wheels for excavation activity. Participate in dinosaur sort and fossil-finding grid activity.	Logical Visual Interpersonal Naturalist Existentialist
Day 6:	
■ Begin reading *Cam Jansen and the Mystery of the Dinosaur Bones.*	Verbal
Day 7:	
■ Continue reading *Cam Jansen.*	Verbal Logical
■ Begin researching class dinosaur: Compsagnathus.	
Day 8:	
■ Read *The Magic School Bus in the Time of the Dinosaurs* together. Learn about time periods and Pangea.	Verbal Logical Interpersonal Existential
■ Continue class research of the class dinosaur; share information found. Begin planning for class presentation of material.	
Day 9:	
■ Finalize class presentation of material and practice.	Verbal Logical Visual Musical Interpersonal
■ Watch selected dinosaur video.	
Day 10:	
■ Unit culmination! Classes gather in library to share material about the dinosaurs with other classes.	Verbal Logical Visual Musical Kinesthetic Interpersonal Existential
■ Have Herbivore/Carnivore/Omnivore Feast.	
Postlesson Follow-Up:	
■ Provide opportunities for extending learning through independent studies about other dinosaurs.	

TABLE 13 ■ "INTEGRATED DINOSAUR RESEARCH" UNIT	
ASSESSMENT:	**INTELLIGENCES:**
■ Research gathered on class dinosaur.	Verbal Logical
■ Comprehension activities from selected readings.	Verbal Logical
■ Completed web of what students learned about dinosaurs.	Verbal Logical Visual Kinesthetic Intrapersonal Naturalist
■ Log of Web sites visited during center times and other completed center materials.	Visual Logical Naturalist
■ Class participation.	Interpersonal

Table 14

"Integrated Dinosaur Research" Unit POMAT Table

POMAT	VL	ML	VS	BK	MR	IE	IA	NT	EX	NOTES
PROCEDURE	✓	✓	✓	✓	✓	✓	✓	✓	✓	KWL charts, reading, excavating, researching, synthesizing information, celebrating learning with other classes
OBJECTIVE	✓	✓	✓	✓	✓	✓		✓		Scientific method, explaining Earth's geology, measurement, directed reading and listening activities
MATERIALS	✓	✓	✓	✓	✓	✓		✓		Literature, poetry, video, measuring tools, excavation materials
ASSESSMENT	✓	✓	✓	✓	✓	✓		✓		Class research, class webs, comprehension activities, completed center materials
TECHNOLOGY	✓	✓	✓	✓	✓			✓		Literature, computer, television, video, excavation tools, Inspiration, Excel, Internet Explorer

VL=VERBAL/LINGUISTIC	**ML=MATHEMATICAL/LOGICAL**	**VS=VISUAL/SPATIAL**
BK=BODILY/KINESTHETIC	**MR=MUSICAL**	**IE=INTERPERSONAL**
IA=INTRAPERSONAL	**NT=NATURALIST**	**EX=EXISTENTIAL**

Chapter 7

Building New Instruction

Having worked through existing lessons, you now have a good frame of reference for developing MI lessons from scratch. From our previous work we know that:

- A lesson cannot be expected to successfully incorporate all nine intelligences at once.

- To accommodate an intelligence, an activity must be in place that uses the intelligence for the explicit purpose of instruction.

- The objective comes first, the identified intelligences come second, and the selected technologies (if any) come third.

- The assessment task for the lesson must have a direct connection to the stated objective and should use intelligences stimulated by the lesson's activity.

- We can check the balance of the intelligences employed in a lesson by using the Wheel of MI Domains (see chapter 2).

Brainstorming Possibilities

The first step in developing an MI lesson plan or unit is to brainstorm the possibilities for connections across the intelligences. This can be especially fruitful when a team of teachers works together, creating a dynamic in which each suggestion stimulates further thinking and the generation of additional possibilities. Start by placing the lesson topic or unit theme in the middle of a page and arranging each of the nine intelligences around its periphery. Focusing on one intelligence at a time, name as many ideas as you can that relate to your topic. In this process there is no need to give detailed descriptions. The best brainstorming sessions are "lightning rounds" in which ideas are rattled off without hesitation. There is time later to decide which of these ideas warrant further consideration.

One digital tool that works well for generating ideas is Inspiration. This semantic mapping tool sets up a main idea and then allows you to generate ideas around it. Its "rapid fire" feature allows you to quickly brainstorm by simply hitting the Enter key each time you come up with a new suggestion. Inspiration also provides for easy manipulation of each item in a map, so that you can rearrange items and show visual connections to related ideas. Figure 4 provides an example of an Inspiration concept map.

After you have generated a variety of ideas, you have the luxury of picking and choosing the activities that will most benefit your lesson or unit. For a lesson, select activities that stimulate three to five intelligences. For a unit, select activities that

Figure 4. Example of an Inspiration Concept Map

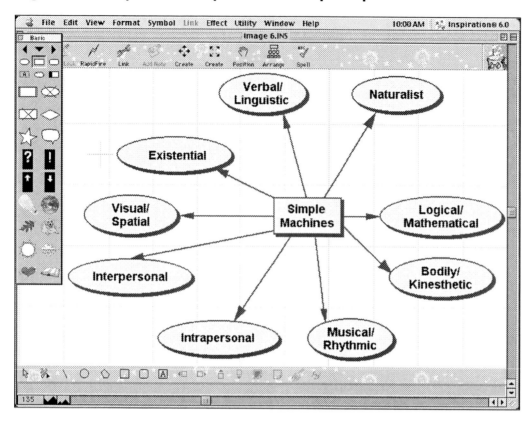

will stimulate all nine intelligences. With these activities selected, you are now ready to write your lesson or unit plan.

An MI Lesson Template

Table 15 offers a template for lessons that incorporate MI and technology. (The CD-ROM accompanying this book also includes this template in the MI_Templates file.) The template follows the key components of a standard lesson but allows for the alignment of the objective with the intelligences and technologies to be used. There is a column for indicating standards (such as ISTE NETS for Students or your state learning standards) and for identifying the intelligences in the Materials and Procedure sections of the plan. Also, a Reflection section allows for specific evaluation of the technology employed with regard to the intelligences and the lesson objective.

Given the flexibility of this template, you can adjust the size of different sections to meet your planning needs. Also, the tabular format of the Objective section allows for a quick visual scan of the intelligences used and their alignment with the objective and technologies. Note that the right-hand column throughout the plan is for listing intelligences as you identify their use. This promotes checking the actual

Table 15

Multiple Intelligences Lesson Template

LESSON TITLE:			TEACHER:
GRADE LEVEL:			
SUBJECT(S):	**DATE:**	**TIME:**	

OBJECTIVE(S):	INTELLIGENCES:	TECHNOLOGIES:	NETS FOR STUDENTS:
MATERIALS:			**INTELLIGENCES:**
PROCEDURE:			**INTELLIGENCES:**
ASSESSMENT:			**INTELLIGENCES:**

REFLECTION:

How did the technologies used accommodate the intelligences you identified?

If the technologies used were not effective, what can you recommend as an alternate application to use with this lesson the next time it is taught?

How did the intelligences identified improve student mastery of the objectives?

Did you observe other intelligences come into play during the lesson? What were they and how did they aid in student learning?

What other intelligences could be included in this lesson?

use of intelligences in the Materials, Procedure, and Assessment sections with those stated in the objective. The Reflection section asks the teacher to evaluate whether the prescribed technologies did indeed stimulate the intended intelligences by focusing on specific examples observed during the lesson. If the technologies used did not meet expectations, the teacher is asked to suggest other technologies that may be more appropriate when the lesson is taught again. Additionally, the Reflection section asks the teacher to evaluate how stimulation of the identified intelligences promoted student learning as defined by the objective, and whether other intelligences also came into play. This provides valuable insight when the teacher next plans to implement this lesson in the classroom.

Let's look at an example of an MI lesson. Mr. Martineau is planning a lesson on spreadsheets for his seventh graders. It is an introductory lesson, but he's not sure of the best way to introduce such a sophisticated productivity tool. He takes a look at the Wheel of MI Domains and determines that an introductory lesson on spreadsheets will have to focus on the logical intelligence as a point of student orientation. Mr. Martineau identifies the logical intelligence in the analytic domain, and then seeks to find an intelligence in the interactive and introspective domains to balance the logical approach. He determines that the visual and kinesthetic intelligences in the introspective domain and the verbal intelligence in the interactive domain will provide a nice balance for his lesson. Mr. Martineau brainstorms activities specifically for these three intelligences and then identifies the activities in stated objectives. In this way he can actually map the objectives to the intelligences.

Objectives

1. The learner will identify, with at least 75% accuracy, a cell, a range of cells, and an auto sum formula. (Logical)

2. The learner will, with at least 80% success, use index cards to visually create a spreadsheet of four columns and five rows. (Visual, Kinesthetic)

3. The learner will, with at least 80% mastery, be able to describe how a spreadsheet uses a formula to complete a simple computation given a range of cells. (Verbal)

Now Mr. Martineau is ready to proceed with the planning of materials, procedure, and assessment for his lesson. By mapping the intelligences to the objectives as a first step in his lesson planning, he ensures that the lesson will be well grounded and will stimulate several different intelligences in the process. Table 16 demonstrates this point.

Table 16

"Introduction to Spreadsheets" Lesson

LESSON TITLE: Introduction to Spreadsheets		**TEACHER:** Martineau	
GRADE LEVEL: 7			
SUBJECT(S): Math **DATE:** March 11, 2002		**TIME:** 10:00-10:50	

OBJECTIVE(S):	INTELLIGENCES:	TECHNOLOGIES:	NETS FOR STUDENTS:
1. The learner will identify, with at least 75% accuracy, a cell, a range of cells, and an auto sum formula by using row and column coordinates.	Intelligences: Logical	Microsoft Excel	1. Basic operations and concepts: Students demonstrate a sound understanding of the nature and operation of technology systems.
2. The learner will, with at least 80% success, use index cards to visually create a spreadsheet of four columns and five rows.	Visual Kinesthetic		
3. The learner will describe, with at least 80% mastery, how a spreadsheet uses a formula to complete a simple computation given a range of cells.	Verbal		3. Technology productivity tools: Students use technology tools to enhance learning and increase productivity.

MATERIALS:	INTELLIGENCES:
Index cards Pencil, paper Microsoft Excel	Visual Kinesthetic Logical

TABLE 16 ■ "INTRODUCTION TO SPREADSHEETS" LESSON	
PROCEDURE:	**INTELLIGENCES:**
Give all students 20 index cards to work with at their desks.	
■ Label cards A1–D5.	Visual
■ Organize cards on desk by rows (1–5) and columns (A–D).	Kinesthetic
■ Lead class on board at front of room and answer questions.	Logical
Turn on LCD projection of blank Excel worksheet.	
■ Compare index cards to cells in the worksheet.	Visual
■ Practice identifying cells by their coordinates.	Logical
Have students turn on their computers.	
■ Launch Excel.	
■ Click on cells and ranges of cells as identified by teacher.	Logical
Type a series of numbers in columns A–D, rows 1–5.	
■ Have students type a series of numbers into their individual worksheets.	Logical
Highlight Column A, rows 1–5, and demonstrate the use of the auto sum button on the toolbar to total the series of numbers for that column.	
■ Have students highlight column A on their worksheets and use the auto sum function to complete the addition of the series of numbers.	Verbal Logical
■ Compare student totals with the teacher's total for column A.	
■ Select the cell that contains the sum for column A and examine the formula bar; discuss how the formula =sum(A1,A5) tells the spreadsheet what function to complete.	
Have students complete columns B–D in the same way.	
■ Ask students to explain the process for finding the sum of a series of numbers in a spreadsheet, using the terms cell, range, toolbar, button, highlight, auto sum, and formula.	Verbal Logical
Turn off computers.	
■ Pass out a sheet of blank paper to each student.	Logical
■ Have students diagram and label a spreadsheet that adds up a sum of five numbers using the auto sum function.	
Collect sheets for evaluation.	

TABLE 16 ■ "INTRODUCTION TO SPREADSHEETS" LESSON

ASSESSMENT:	INTELLIGENCES:
Students identify, with 80% accuracy, cell coordinates using index cards.	Visual Kinesthetic
Students identify spreadsheet coordinates and correctly use the auto sum feature 3 out of 4 times.	Logical
Learners explain the process of using the auto sum function for finding the sum of a series of numbers with correct terminology at least 4 out of 5 times.	Verbal Logical

REFLECTION:

How did the technologies used accommodate the intelligences you intended?

Excel strongly reinforced the logical intelligence by providing a structure for lining up numbers and creating an elementary formula.

If the technologies used were not effective, can you recommend an alternate application to use with this lesson the next time it is taught?

None

How did the intelligences identified improve student mastery of the objective(s)?

Students who do not usually do well on logical tasks were able to see the format of a spreadsheet. The verbal components helped students to internalize and express their understanding of the spreadsheet algorithm.

Did you observe other intelligences come into play during the lesson? What were they and how did they aid in student learning?

Yes. The musical intelligence came into play as students recognized a repeated pattern in adding each column. Comparing formulas for each column also aided in understanding of the spreadsheet auto sum function.

What other intelligences could be included in this lesson?

Intrapersonal—Evaluating others' explanations of spreadsheet functions.

Interpersonal—Group work constructing spreadsheets.

Here's a second example. Ms. Godwin is going to teach her students research skills using digital multimedia resources. Table 17 shows how she stimulates a variety of intelligences to make this year's lesson as effective as it can be.

Table 17

"Information Skills" Lesson

LESSON TITLE: Information Skills		TEACHER: Sherri Godwin East Clayton Elementary School Clayton, North Carolina	
GRADE LEVEL: 3–4			
SUBJECT(S): Language Arts DATE: March 30, 2003		TIME: 1:15–2:30	

OBJECTIVE(S):	INTELLIGENCES:	TECHNOLOGIES:	NETS FOR STUDENTS:
1. Students will learn to use multimedia to access information for recreational and informational purposes.	Verbal Logical	Library information system	1. Basic operations and concepts: Students are proficient in the use of technology.
2. Students will search information using Grolier's Multimedia Encyclopedia.	Visual Musical	CD–ROM	2. Social, ethical, and human issues: Students practice responsible use of technology systems, information and software.
3. Students will listen to and interact with multimedia by using Living Books.	Visual Musical	CD–ROM	
4. Students will use Internet resources available through www.yahooligans.com.	Verbal Naturalist	Browser	
MATERIALS: Printouts of digital sources Art supplies		**INTELLIGENCES:** Verbal Visual Kinesthetic	5. Technology research tools: Students use technology to locate, evaluate and collect information from a variety of sources.

TABLE 17 ■ "INFORMATION SKILLS" LESSON	
PROCEDURE:	**INTELLIGENCES:**
Working in groups of two, students will complete the following tasks:	Interpersonal
Grolier's Multimedia Encyclopedia	
■ Students will click on the GME icon.	
■ Students will choose one of the following topics: Dog Library Lindbergh's Transatlantic Flight North Carolina Facts About Symphony	Intrapersonal
■ Students will visit the Related Media and Sound sections.	Visual, Musical
■ Students will click on links related to pictures or sound.	
■ Students will enlarge pictures.	
■ Students will listen to sounds.	
■ Students will save and print information they wish to share.	
Living Books	
■ Students will choose one of the following: *Arthur's Computer Adventure* *The Cat in the Hat* *Just Grandma and Me* *Shelia Rae, the Brave* *The Tortoise and the Hare*	Intrapersonal
■ Students will complete the activities associated with one of the Living Books. Some activities are completed away from the computer with writing or art activities.	Verbal Visual Musical
■ Students will save and print their work.	
Yahooligans	Naturalist
■ Students will access the Internet and type in www.yahooligans.com.	
■ Students will find the School Bell heading and click the Language Arts link.	
■ Students will scroll down to Word Games.	
■ Students will click Hangman.	Verbal
■ Students play several rounds of this game to test their wits.	
■ Students will scroll down to Wacky Web Tales.	
■ Students will save and print their stories.	

TABLE 17 ■ "INFORMATION SKILLS" LESSON

ASSESSMENT:	INTELLIGENCES:
Students will have a collection of materials in hard copy from three different digital sources.	Visual
Students will be able to describe the steps for accessing each source by referencing the printouts they have from the lesson.	Verbal, Logical
Students will be able to classify printouts from each source based on the information on the printouts from the lesson.	Naturalist

REFLECTION:

How did the technologies used accommodate the intelligences you intended?

The digital resources stimulated the Verbal, Logical, Visual, Musical, and Naturalist intelligences.

If the technologies used were not effective, can you recommend an alternate application to use with this lesson the next time it is taught?

None

How did the intelligences identified improve student mastery of the objective(s)?

They especially provided the opportunity for students to complete an activity using each resource and printing out a finished product. This allowed extended time for stimulating the nontraditional visual and musical intelligences for research.

Did you observe other intelligences come into play during the lesson? What were they and how did they aid in student learning?

Yes. The Kinesthetic intelligence came into play as students completed art activities related to the Living Books.

What other intelligences could be included in this lesson?

Existential—Have students locate and respond to works of art.

By brainstorming possibilities for the different intelligences and then using the MI lesson plan template, teachers can develop threads of continuity through their lesson plans for objectives, intelligences, and technologies.

An MI Unit Template

Units of instruction can be developed with the intelligences in mind in the same way. Rather than brainstorming activities for objectives, though, you can generate ideas for unit goals. Table 18 shows the template for mapping the goals to intelligences and technologies. (The CD-ROM accompanying this book also contains the MI Unit template in the MI_Templates file.)

Table 18

Multiple Intelligences Unit Template

UNIT TITLE:			TEACHER:
GRADE LEVEL:			
SUBJECT(S):			TIME FRAME:
OBJECTIVE(S):	INTELLIGENCES:	TECHNOLOGIES:	NETS FOR STUDENTS:
MATERIALS:			INTELLIGENCES:
DAILY TASKS:			INTELLIGENCES:
ASSESSMENT:			INTELLIGENCES:

Table 19 shows how Ms. English employed this format to develop an elections unit using technology and the intelligences.

Choosing to integrate MI and technology into this study unit expands the possibilities for students because they are not only learning about the electoral process but are also actually experiencing it in a way that uses all nine intelligences. You can tell just by reading over Ms. English's plan that her students will be immersed in a series of learning experiences so engrossing and so memorable that the learning will be meaningful and retained.

Table 19

"Presidential Elections" Unit

UNIT TITLE: Presidential Elections	TEACHER: Betty Jo English
GRADE LEVEL: 2	The Pruden Center for Industry and Technology Suffolk, Virginia
SUBJECT(S): Computer Applications	TIME FRAME: 6 weeks

OBJECTIVE(S):	INTELLIGENCES:	TECHNOLOGIES:	NETS FOR STUDENTS:
1. To use graphic software to create and/or manipulate graphics/pictures.	Visual Kinesthetic	Draw	1. Students are proficient in the use of technology.
2. To reinforce a knowledge of United States geography.	Existential	Text WWW CD-ROM	2. Students develop positive attitudes toward technology uses that support lifelong learning.
3. To use electronic spreadsheet software to record and analyze data through graphs.	Logical Visual Musical	Excel	3. Students use technology tools to enhance learning and increase productivity.
4. To use database software to create a voter registration record, file, and report.	Verbal Logical Naturalist	Access	
5. To use desktop-publishing techniques to create a variety of documents.	Verbal Visual	Publisher	4. Students use a variety of media and formats to communicate information.
6. To use various research techniques.	Verbal Logical	WWW CD-ROM	5. Students use technology to locate, evaluate and collect information from a variety of sources.

TABLE 19 ■ "PRESIDENTIAL ELECTIONS" UNIT			
OBJECTIVES:	**INTELLIGENCES:**	**TECHNOLOGIES:**	**NETS FOR STUDENTS:**
7. To increase knowledge of the process of the election of the President of the United States.	Logical Intrapersonal Interpersonal	WWW CD-ROM Videotape	6. Students use technology resources for solving problems and making informed decisions.

MATERIALS:	**INTELLIGENCES:**
Voter registration form	Interpersonal
Sample presidential ballot	Intrapersonal
Legal-size printer paper	Visual
Masking tape	Kinesthetic
Audio tape	Musical
Brochure paper	Visual
Hardware:	
Networked computers with Internet connection	Existential
Color printers	Visual
Digital camera	Visual
Scanner	Visual
Audio tape recorder	Musical
Software:	
Desktop-publishing software	Verbal/Visual
Electronic spreadsheet software	Logical/Visual
Desktop presentation software	Logical/Naturalist
Graphic/draw software	Visual/Kinesthetic
HTML editor	Visual/Kinesthetic
Internet browser	Visual/Interpersonal
Web Sites:	
Web White & Blue: www.webwhiteblue.org	Intrapersonal
Elections USA:	Existential
www.geocities.com/CapitolHill/6228/pres2000/index.html	
The Center for Responsive Politics:	Intrapersonal
www.opensecrets.org/2000elect/index/AllCands.htm	
ABC News Politics: http://abcnews.go.com/sections/politics/	Existential
Vote Net: www.votenet.com	Interpersonal
CNN Election News: http://cnn.com/ELECTION/2000/	Existential
Washington Post Election Coverage:	Existential
www.washingtonpost.com/wp-dyn/politics/elections/2000/	

TABLE 19 ■ "PRESIDENTIAL ELECTIONS" UNIT

MATERIALS:	INTELLIGENCES:
Project Vote Smart: www.vote-smart.org	Intrapersonal
Project Vote Smart Youth Inclusion: www.vote-smart.org/yip/	Intrapersonal
C-SPAN Election 2000 Links: www.c-span.org/campaign2000/ links.asp	Existential
U.S. Electoral College Home Page: www.nara.gov/fedreg/ echmpge.html	Logical/Musical
Election 2000 People Parties Process: www.teachersfirst.com/election/index.htm	Interpersonal
The Gallop Poll: www.gallup.com/index.html	Logical/Musical
Video Resources: PBS series The American President C-SPAN current activities programming Videotaped campaign ads	Verbal/Visual

DAILY TASKS:	INTELLIGENCES:
Preparation:	
Group discussion of steps in selecting a president, primaries, conventions, polls, and debates	Verbal Interpersonal Intrapersonal Existential
Activities:	
1. Steps in Selecting a President	Logical Interpersonal Visual
After a whole-class discussion of the steps and small-group research on the Internet about primaries and conventions, the students will work in groups of two using desktop-publishing or graphic software to create a flowchart of the steps OR a graphic of the campaign trail.	
2. Political Vocabulary	Verbal Logical
Students will be given a list of political vocabulary words. Working in small groups, the students will use various research materials to locate appropriate definitions for each word.	
Students will use desktop-publishing software to create a crossword puzzle using their definitions. Puzzles will be printed and shared with U.S. government teachers for classroom use.	
3. Registering to Vote	Verbal Logical Interpersonal Naturalist Existential
Invite the local voter registrar as a guest speaker to discuss: (a) who may register to vote and (b) methods of voter registration in Virginia.	

TABLE 19 ■ "PRESIDENTIAL ELECTIONS" UNIT	
DAILY TASKS:	**INTELLIGENCES:**
After reviewing actual voter registration forms, students will use desktop-publishing software to create a mock voter registration form for use in the schoolwide election.	
Students will work in small groups to visit each classroom to have students register for the mock election.	
Using database software, create a database of registered voters for the mock election. Create a report for use on Election Day to verify voter registration.	
4. Who Are the Candidates?	Verbal Visual
In small groups, students will use the Internet to research the main candidates for President and Vice-President.	
Students will use research results to create a candidate biography in one of the following modes: (a) desktop presentation, (b) Web page, (c) brochure, (d) newsletter.	
5. What Are the Issues?	Verbal Intrapersonal Interpersonal Naturalist Existential
Students will bring in news articles on a weekly basis covering the issues and the candidates' views or positions. Conduct a whole-class oral discussion of the articles. Display the articles in the classroom for reference.	
In small groups, develop the layout for a comparison table, chart, or grid on the candidates' views on at least eight major issues.	
Use appropriate software to generate the comparison table, chart, or grid.	
6. Candidates on the Road	Verbal Logical Visual Intrapersonal Interpersonal
Students will be divided into teams by party. Each team will use the newspaper, television news, or Internet for a daily check of where the candidates for their party are campaigning. Using a U.S. map graphic and graphics software, students will plot the movements of the candidates during the campaign.	
Conduct a class discussion of why some states have more campaigning activity. Have students discuss why they think that candidates are campaigning more in these states.	
7. Campaign Ads	Verbal Visual Musical Intrapersonal Interpersonal Visual
The whole class will view videos of various campaign ads. Conduct a class discussion of the effects of negative ads.	
Use desktop-publishing software to create campaign posters	

TABLE 19 ■ "PRESIDENTIAL ELECTIONS" UNIT	
DAILY TASKS:	**INTELLIGENCES:**
for candidates. Use posters in hallways for the mock election. OR Write and record a radio campaign ad. OR Write and use desktop presentation software to create a television campaign ad.	
8. The Ballot After reviewing a sample presidential ballot, students will use desktop-publishing software to create an election ballot for the schoolwide mock election. The class will vote for the ballot to be used for the election. Use a copying machine to produce enough ballots for the number of registered voters.	Intrapersonal Kinesthetic
9. The Electoral College Working in small groups, students will use the Internet or other current reference sources to determine the number of electoral votes for each state. Students will use electronic spreadsheet software to create a spreadsheet listing each state and the number of electoral votes. This spreadsheet will be saved for use after the actual election.	Logical Naturalist
10. Stage a Mock Election The class will designate each class as a specific state for Electoral College purposes. Students will modify their Electoral College spreadsheet with this information. On Election Day, students will go to each class, check the registration database report to verify the student has registered to vote, distribute a ballot, and have students return it to the ballot box. The class will count the ballots by class. A student recorder will draw a graph on the chalkboard and record results by class. Students will then modify their Electoral College spreadsheet showing popular vote by class (state). Using the Electoral College spreadsheet, students will add columns for each candidate to record the allocation of electoral votes received. This data will be used to create a pie chart displaying Electoral College results.	Logical Visual Interpersonal Existential

TABLE 19 ■ "PRESIDENTIAL ELECTIONS" UNIT	
DAILY TASKS:	**INTELLIGENCES:**
11. After the Vote The day after the election, students will create another electronic spreadsheet using the Electoral College data. Students will use the morning newspaper or the Internet to record the national election results. The class will create a pie chart of the results. Students will compare the mock election results with the actual election results. Conduct a class discussion of how these compare and why.	Verbal Logical Visual Musical Naturalist Existential
Postlesson Follow-Up: Conduct a group discussion of election results. Analyze why the students think voters made their decision. What became the major issue of the campaign?	Verbal Logical Visual Musical Intrapersonal Interpersonal Naturalist Existential
ASSESSMENT:	**INTELLIGENCES:**
Students will be asked to organize each product produced during the unit into a unit portfolio. Students will be graded using a rubric	Verbal Logical Visual Musical Kinesthetic Intrapersonal Interpersonal Naturalist Existential

Table 20 demonstrates how Carol LaVallee tried to create similar learning connections for her students in a science unit for her second graders. Carol mapped from her state standards for learning to the intelligences and then mapped the technologies to specific intelligences in the Materials section of her plan. The result is a unit that meets the criteria set forth by the state of Florida—and the criteria set forth by the human mind. What student wouldn't want to be part of the rich, gratifying learning environment in Carol's classroom?

Table 20

"Amazon Rainforest" Unit

UNIT TITLE: Amazon Rainforest		TEACHER: Carol LaVallee Venice Area Middle School Venice, Florida	
GRADE LEVEL: 2–3			
SUBJECT(S): Self-Motivated Geography, History, World Cultures, Economics		TIME FRAME: 6 weeks	
OBJECTIVE(S):	**INTELLIGENCES:**	**TECHNOLOGIES:**	**FLORIDA STATE STANDARDS:**
Students will describe ways regions are interconnected and interdependent.	Verbal Logical Visual	Video Web page	2.1.3
Students will compare and contrast ways various cultures use similar resources and environments.	Verbal Logical Musical Naturalist Existential	Draw/Paint program	2.1.4
Students will recognize the environmental consequences resulting from people changing the physical environment.	Verbal Logical Musical Intrapersonal Naturalist Existential	Web site	2.1.5
Students will describe how various geofeatures have influenced the development and interaction of Latin American cultures.	Verbal Logical Musical Naturalist Existential Visual	Web site	2.3.4

TABLE 20 ■ "AMAZON RAINFOREST" UNIT

OBJECTIVE(S):	INTELLIGENCES:	TECHNOLOGIES:	FLORIDA STATE STANDARDS:
Students will recognize examples of the arts and architecture that reflect the various cultures in Latin America.	Visual Musical Intrapersonal Naturalist Existential	Web site	3.3.5
Students will describe major characteristics and accomplishments of the Mayan and Aztec civilizations.	Verbal Intrapersonal Existential	Web site	4.2.1
Students will analyze effects of European rule in Latin America.	Verbal Logical Intrapersonal Interpersonal Existential	Oral presentation	4.2.2
Students will describe the struggle for independence of Latin American nations.	Verbal Intrapersonal Interpersonal Existential	Oral presentation	4.2.3
Students will describe current issues that affect political, social, and economic systems.	Verbal Intrapersonal Interpersonal Existential	Oral presentation	4.2.6

MATERIALS:	INTELLIGENCES:
Hardware:	
Computer	Kinesthetic
Digital camera	Visual
Video camera	Visual
Cassette/CD player	Musical
Overhead	Visual
VCR	Visual/Musical
Microphone	Verbal/Musical
Software:	
CD-ROM (encyclopedia, atlas)	Verbal/Logical
Word processor (Appleworks)	Verbal

TABLE 20 ■ "AMAZON RAINFOREST" UNIT	
MATERIALS:	**INTELLIGENCES:**
Drawing, painting (Appleworks)	Visual/Kinesthetic
Spreadsheet (Appleworks)	Logical/Visual
Web page editor (Appleworks)	Visual/Verbal
Avid Cinema	Visual/Verbal
HyperStudio	Visual/Kinesthetic
Fireworks2 (photo/imaging)	Visual/Kinesthetic
Other Materials:	
Floppy disk	Naturalist
Video cassettes	Visual
Tape cassettes	Musical
Art supplies	Kinesthetic
DAILY TASKS:	**INTELLIGENCES:**
Prelesson Class Preparation:	
The teacher makes up centers or stations. Each station is titled with the topic and one of Bloom's taxonomies, for example, Rainforest Knowledge, Rainforest Comprehension, Rainforest Application. At these stations, the teacher supplies instructions for students. Students choose how they are going to present their project and choose their own assessment. Students are given a list of MI-based assessments acceptable to the teacher. Student will choose which assessment he or she will present to the class, for example, skit, Web page, poster, song, essay, debate, photo essay, editorial. Students will also make a class rubric with teacher input.	
Procedure:	
Students are given packet of the same instructions found at stations a week before to take home and look over with parents. (Verbal, Intrapersonal)	
Students need to decide which station they will start at. However, students still need to complete all stations. (This way, no one is held back; self-motivators can move ahead while teacher motivators can receive guidance from a facilitator.) (Intrapersonal)	
At the stations, students will find a task to fulfill. Then the students choose how to fulfill the task at the stations with teacher suggestions of MI activities. (Verbal, Logical)	
Students will then work independently.	

TABLE 20 ■ "AMAZON RAINFOREST" UNIT	
DAILY TASKS:	**INTELLIGENCES:**
Activities:	
Reading from a textbook or magazine, writing a journal entry, recording a journal entry on a cassette.	Verbal
Solve the issue at Ecotourism Game Introduction: www.eduweb.com/ecotourism/eco1.html	Logical
Watch a movie on the Amazon rainforest. Create a chart or graph of rainforest depletion.	Visual Logical Naturalist
Listen to rainforest audioclips at Nature Net: www.naturenet.com.br/eng.htm	Musical
Videotape a student portraying an Amazon news reporter. Play game on CD–ROM titled "Amazon Trail."	Interpersonal Intrapersonal
Paint a rainforest image and give it a name or title.	Kinesthetic Intrapersonal
Make a rainforest plant or animal from construction paper.	Kinesthetic
Research at ITL Rainforest Lesson Web page: http://scrtec.org/track/tracks/f10668.html	Verbal Naturalist
Review the Rainforest Alliance Home Page and explain what is being done today: www.rainforest-alliance.org	Existential
Postlesson Follow-Up: After all presentations are completed, the teacher creates a quiz on the Internet for students to take at home and complete that evening or at school the next day.	
ASSESSMENT:	**INTELLIGENCES:**
Skit, debate, or oral report	Verbal
Chronology of the growth of a rainforest, statistics	Logical
Video, commercial, Web page, poster, photo essay	Visual
Song lyric, music video, plant patterns	Musical
Painting, clay sculpture, drawing, building a model of a rainforest, cooking recipes from native rainforest lands	Kinesthetic
Lead a discussion	Verbal Interpersonal
Present concerns on vanishing rainforests	Intrapersonal
Present rainforest flora and fauna, categorize rainforests	Naturalist
Examine the role of the rainforests in human survival	Existential
At the end of two weeks, students will use class rubric as they present their projects to the class while teacher and students fill out rubric during presentation.	Intrapersonal

Creating new lessons and units of instruction based on Gardner's theory is a process that requires much reflection and attention to instructional design. But the reward is in the resulting quality of instruction you can provide to your students and the kinds of learning experiences they will keep with them for their entire lifetime.

Reflections

❶ How do you determine what is a reasonable number of intelligences for a lesson to accommodate?

❷ Should a unit of instruction be designed to stimulate all the intelligences? Why or why not?

❸ When is it more beneficial to accommodate the intelligences using industrial technologies? When is it more beneficial to use digital technologies? Why do you think so?

❹ The two lesson examples in this chapter focus on content, with technology use as incidental to the lesson. Other examples have taught technology for technology's sake. Is one approach more valid than the other? Why?

Chapter 8

Becoming a Technoconstructivist

The human variable in integrating MI theory into instruction is perhaps the most important. Many new approaches to instruction have come down the road with great fanfare, only to continue traveling right out of town until they disappeared on the horizon. Ask a veteran teacher what he or she thinks about the latest and greatest innovation in education, and that teacher will tell you stories of similar approaches that were touted 15 or 20 years ago. What goes around comes around in education. There is rarely anything new under the sun.

So when something reinvents the fundamental structure of society the way digital technology does, people sit up and take notice. And even if some educators are not thrilled with the idea of having to master the new technologies as part of their instructional expertise, they cannot ignore the money being spent on hardware, software, and training (and the community expectations) to do just that. In certain states, teacher certification is already being linked to the mastery of technology proficiencies. Reality has hit home as educators choose to either update their training or leave the profession.

Educational Reform

When a new innovation is assimilated into an institution like public education, it takes on many forces already in place. There are educational reform movements requiring teachers to document and improve the quality of the education children receive. There are pressures from special interest groups who want emphasis placed on literacy, science, math, or social studies areas of the curriculum. Teachers are also preoccupied with doing all they can to promote student success on state standardized achievement tests.

Meanwhile, the educational dollar will stretch only so far. Thus, priorities are made and technology falls into place based on the values and attitudes held by local administrators. If you're working in a district where technology receives major emphasis, then technology becomes your imperative. If you're working in a district where basic skills and core curriculum values are emphasized first and foremost, technology, with its powerful applications to higher order thinking, may not be high on your list of professional priorities.

For the majority of educators who do not work in a district adopting either extreme, the choice is made in individual classrooms. Based on availability of technology, sufficient training in using what's available, and the value a teacher places on technology as an instructional tool, the level of access to technology that students receive is determined by teachers on a classroom-by-classroom basis. The typical teacher wants to incorporate technology as he or she sees fit. This leaves a wide-open technology playing field, but it limits student use of technology to applications determined by the teacher. For example, in a single school, all six fourth-grade classes may be studying the solar system at the same time. Three teachers may have their students creating three-dimensional working models of the relationship among the Sun, Earth, and Moon. One of these three teachers may actually bookmark a short list of excellent Web sites for student research, including a NASA Ask-an-Expert site, sites with pictures taken in space and transmitted to Earth, and several sites that use current Web technologies to present interactive animations of the solar system and its phenomena.

While the other two teachers mentioned have their students use Styrofoam and papier-mâché, respectively, to create their models, our technology-connected teacher asks groups of four students to create digital multimedia presentations that will demonstrate working models of the Sun, Earth, and Moon. She also provides her students with links to vocabulary and external links to Web resources offering more information on the subject. Her students have expressed interest in creating interactive quizzes at the end of their presentations, and the teacher in question has already contacted the school Web master about posting these finished products on the school Web site to share with the larger community. Only a small number of children from the six fourth-grade classes will have the opportunity to study the solar system using digital technology because only one of the six teachers has made it a priority in her instruction.

Then again, many teachers are so sensitive to current trends in accountability and documentation of student learning that they shy away from technology as just another approach to instruction. "How can we possibly spend a lot of time on computer applications," they wonder, "when there is so much content to cover before state testing that we'll be lucky if these kids are ready?" Others who are required to make time for computers in instruction still resist, saying, "All these higher level applications are fine, but they aren't going to help my kids fill in the bubbles correctly on standardized tests. What they need is more drill on skills!"

These pressures are very real. In some areas teachers are actually in danger of losing their jobs if a set percentage of students do not pass these tests every spring. So there is a need to do some soul searching among ourselves. Do we sincerely believe that the most effective way to prepare children for standardized tests is to offer instruction that panders to lower levels of thinking?

The Story of Jamie

Consider the story of Jamie, a young man I taught in fourth grade just as the Virginia Standards of Learning (SOL) tests were being rolled out statewide. Jamie was functioning below grade level in language arts and mathematics, and he received daily instruction from a specialist in both areas to supplement his regular classroom work. Coming from a disadvantaged home, Jamie did not have a lot of the material things other students owned; and living a little less than an hour from our nation's capital, he had not been exposed to any of its cultural riches. Jamie's cumulative record read all too familiar to this veteran teacher of 14 years. His standardized test scores were extremely low and his annual report card grades were consistent from year to year. Jamie also had regular discipline problems with peers and teachers because he did not like school.

This was the first year that Virginia schools were expected to have at least 70% of their students pass a state SOL test on Virginia. All five of us teaching fourth grade in the school felt under the gun to do everything we could for each of our students to cover 400 years of Virginia history, including economics, government, and current events.

As we met to plan at the beginning of the year, three of the teachers were sure that they wanted to hit social studies hard with lots of names, dates, places, and map skills, using as many textbooks, worksheets, homework assignments, and quizzes as they could muster for the year. While I was aware that this was a strongly traditional way to go, I wasn't sure that I would be able to say that the students had mastered anything more than rote memorization by testing time in May. I knew there had to be other ways to make this mountain of information meaningful to them.

A teammate joined me in my search for something just as comprehensive but more supportive of students in the different ways children learn. We came up with a cache of instructional approaches for the year that the two of us planned to work on together.

That year my students built a wigwam, researched colonial crafts, conducted a colonial day, performed a musical play in the tradition of 1776, participated in the construction of a Web site on the achievements of Thomas Jefferson, drilled with mop handles over their shoulders in the April mud while singing Civil War songs, used the local newspaper in weekly activities to learn about government and current events, and competed weekly against our rival class in the SOL Olympics (we fondly referred to it as the "SOLympics") to challenge one another in the mastery of Virginia history.

When May rolled around, all five classes took the Virginia SOL Social Studies test. Not one of the five teachers knew how well our kids would test that first year. We all showed deference to one another's methods and supported one another as we waited for the test results to come back.

There was a lot of soul searching on my part during the weeks we waited for the results. What if the drill-and-practice approach worked more successfully? Even worse, what if our highly visible efforts to use more learner-centered approaches to instruction failed and everyone knew it? But it was too late to turn back. The testing was done, the work was turned in, and the chips were going to fall where they may.

When the test scores came back, the results were riveting. My teammate and I had the only two classes out of the five in which at least 70% of the students passed the test. Granted, both classes scored in the low 70s, but we had gotten over the bar set by the state. This was wonderful validation for our instincts that there had to be a better way to cover such a huge volume of material successfully. As I looked more closely at each of my student's scores, I was glad to see that almost everyone scored relatively close to my expectations. Even those who didn't pass the test did well enough that I knew they had grown a lot during the year. The evidence clearly indicated that each student gave it his or her very best effort.

Then I came to Jamie's score sheet. I was astounded. Here was this young man just struggling to meet minimum requirements for promotion at each grade level, and he had scored in the 99th percentile on the test! I went over the way the scores broke down for him, and time and time again he was able to determine the correct answer for each test item and outscore every other student in my class!

I thought about this in amazement. How could someone who struggled with reading comprehension be able to do so well on a standardized test? As I looked back over the year, I remembered Jamie's participation in all of our activities built around our Virginia studies. Verbally he was always able to master the material, and he was quite a ham during our production of our colonial-era play and our weekly SOLympics competitions. Also, he loved the Civil War drilling, the singing, the class wigwam, and the study of Jefferson.

I spoke with his Chapter 1 teacher to get her take on his success, and she informed me that she was not at all surprised because in her room Jamie had truly blossomed as a reader that year. She had been working with him since kindergarten, and she was amazed at how his attitude toward school had changed and how he was finally able to make the act of reading "click" for himself. As I put together the big picture of Jamie's year, my amazement subsided and I began to be humbled by the momentous achievements he had accomplished.

I will never forget the lessons I learned that year. Sure, I had always subscribed to developmentally appropriate practice and multimodal learning. I always talked a good game and wanted to implement as much of it as I could. But there was always a shadow of doubt cast upon my convictions by colleagues who did not subscribe to such child-centered practices.

For me, Jamie's accomplishments were all the validation I needed. I knew now that everything that made sense to me about teaching and learning actually did work. Even under strong pressures to skill and drill, teaching to all children at higher levels of thinking won out. I believe that all teachers would be willing to let go of their skills checklists and worksheets if they didn't feel such pressure to be accountable for state standards. After all, most of us didn't get into teaching for the money. We got into teaching to see that spark in children when they get excited about new learning. That's what it's all about.

The Four-Tier Model

Technology is a different story, though. Many teachers entered the profession long before the microcomputer appeared in the schools. Technology has been thrust upon them as one more requirement they never agreed to when they first entered the classroom. How do teachers respond to the challenge of integrating technology into their existing instructional practices? Scott Noon, of Classroom Connect, examined this question and came up with the four-tier model of teacher training in technology summarized in Table 21. Each tier of the model demonstrates an identifiable stage in teacher technology proficiency. The model holds implications for how teachers learn to use technology and the journey they make in the process. Let's take a look at Noon's model.

Table 21

Noon's Four-Tier Model of Technological Proficiency for Teachers

STAGE	DESCRIPTION	EXAMPLES
PRELITERATE	Not yet using technology for personal or instructional purposes.	Traditional media and materials
TECHNOCRAT	Experimenting with technology but unsure of its overall dependability and usefulness.	Demonstration station with LCD projector, computer lab, learning station with computer
TECHNOTRADITIONALIST	Using technology proficiently to accomplish traditional classroom tasks.	Word-processing lesson plans, electronic gradebook, e-mail, digital slideshow
TECHNOCONSTRUCTIVIST	Using technology to completely change approaches to teaching and learning in the classroom.	Online projects, virtual field trips, WebQuests, digital portfolios, virtual classrooms

The Preliterate User

This is where we all begin. We are aware of technology's presence in our buildings, even in our classrooms, but we do not have the training, experience, or confidence to use the technology. The teacher that fits in this category has yet to have an e-mail account, use a word processor, or even find a piece of appropriate software that he or she can use with students to enrich instruction. Perhaps technology seems like another entire body of knowledge that there just isn't time to master. Or perhaps technology seems like a lot of fluff that gets in the way of good old honest instructional time on task.

For each teacher the reasons may certainly be different, but the overwhelming response I hear from groups of teachers no matter where I go is, "We just haven't had the training we need to know how to make good use of all the hardware and software that's been purchased for us to use."

The institution of education is very quick to throw money at an issue or innovation and very quick to move on to other trendy ideas without giving invested initiatives time to fully realize their potential. Teachers are telling us that this is the danger technology is facing in the schools if they don't have the funds for the training needed to make the technology puzzle complete. There are few preliterate users by choice. No one wants to be left behind. And since we all start at this point, perhaps that is the impetus that compels us to move forward and become more proficient with technology. Still, how do we move on without the prerequisite training?

The Technocrat

This second tier of Noon's model identifies a critical point in teacher technology training. The teachers in this category have ventured out to learn how to use an LCD projector connected to a demonstration computer station. They have made the effort to identify instructional applications that students can successfully use in the computer lab. At the high end of this tier, teachers even dabble in new, more advanced applications to invigorate themselves.

The main characteristic of this category, though, is that the teacher is preoccupied with the technical aspects of technology. How do I turn it on? What do I do if the bulb burns out while I'm presenting to my entire class? What if the server is down and I have 25 children unable to complete the online task I had planned?

Of course, the only way to answer these questions is to learn from experience. Technology always offers the possibility of glitches and unforeseen mishaps. High-end users understand this, and have learned to face their fears, learn the tricks of the trade, and have a Plan B handy whenever technology is going to be used. By giving teachers the time and support necessary to be able to grow as a technocrat, we are investing in the long-term goal of having teachers who will truly use technology because they are no longer afraid of it.

I believe that once they see past their fears, they can set their sights on the possibilities for technology enriching their lives both personally and professionally.

The Technotraditionalist

At the third tier, Noon recognizes the stage the majority of teachers reach at some point. Technology is seen as an inherent good thing in instruction, and it can be used in a variety of ways around the classroom. Teachers at this level often create word-processing templates so they can write their lesson plans in an easy-to-use format. Likewise, technotraditionalist teachers use spreadsheets to create seating charts and electronic grade books.

The teachers at this level are finally high-end users, but they use technology to complete the same tasks they have traditionally always accomplished as teachers. Is there anything wrong with that? No! It is an important stage in the development of the technology-savvy teacher. Still, if we are using technology to go about our business keeping track of lunch counts and typing reports to hang on the wall, how far have we really come? Yes, it's more efficient to set up a database to make mailing labels you can use all year for your students, but you're still holding on to the traditional ways of looking at instruction.

If technology is going to be a true agent for change in education (and this remains to be seen), educators at all levels are going to have to be willing to ask themselves a lot of fundamental questions about why they still do things as they always have. Perhaps some of our preconceptions have to do with growing up in the Industrial Age, when many Digital Age possibilities were not yet available. If technology holds new possibilities for solving traditional problems, then we may have to rethink our assumptions and be willing to go beyond traditionalist uses of technology.

The Technoconstructivist

The technoconstructivist occupies the highest tier in Noon's model. Here, teachers not only integrate the affordances of technology that fit into the traditional view of instruction, but they are also willing to reshape that view and carve out new territory for their classrooms. In fact, technoconstructivists not only use technology as an instructional tool, but they also employ it to transform the classroom into a new and different learning environment for students.

In the technoconstructivist classroom students and teachers use Web resources, electronic mail, online collaborative projects, synchronous Web-based events, virtual field trips, WebQuests, multimedia presentations, virtual classrooms, interactive simulations, and much, much more. As the Internet transports the physical four walls of the classroom past the traditional boundaries of time, space, and money, students are able to achieve higher levels of thinking, use real-world applications, and collaborate with experts and other learners from around the world.

The result is a learning revolution, where the teacher becomes a facilitator for all the possibilities in learning about the world around us, both virtual and otherwise. The technoconstructivist is at the highest level of technological proficiency for teachers, and we must all aspire to being a technoconstructivist if we are going to realize technology's full potential for our students.

The question we each must ask ourselves is, "Is technology just another tool for instruction?" If the answer is yes, then we know we have yet to consider technology as much more than another piece of equipment in our classrooms. Is that okay? Yes. But the potential for making full use of technology only takes place when we hear ourselves saying, "No, technology is not just another tool for instruction!" because at that moment we are willing to let go of all our preconceived notions and see all the possibilities for our students.

Now consider MI theory in light of Noon's model. How does a teacher use MI with technology in any of the first three tiers? Perhaps one can argue that at the technotraditionalist level teachers are capable of at least accommodating several intelligences at once, perhaps without even realizing it.

While I would concede that point, I would counter by asking, "Is this what we want for good instruction, hitting on effective strategies without possibly even realizing we have done so?" No, good instruction has always been a well-honed craft with reflective practitioners meeting their objectives. Why settle for a hit-

and-miss model of learning when Gardner and Noon give us such practical, empirical models to use? In order to integrate MI theory and technology into instruction, one must aspire to become a technoconstructivist. Only at this level can teachers truly realize the full potential of every student in their charge.

Figure 5 shows how one teacher, Dana, transformed her seventh-graders' study of the nervous system into a celebration of learning through different technologies. Table 22 shows the resulting lesson plan.

Dana is a blossoming technoconstructivist. Her varied classroom activities and use of technology to accomplish deeper student understanding speak well of her determination to make everyday learning a memorable event in her classroom.

Figure 5. Lesson Plan Flowchart Example

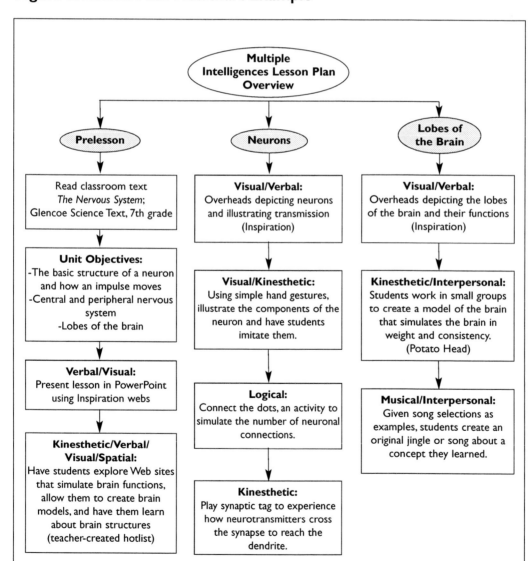

Table 22

"Our Brain—The 3-Pound Wonder" Lesson

LESSON TITLE: Our Brain—The 3-Pound Wonder			TEACHER: Dana Topham
GRADE LEVEL: 7–8			Ascension Day School Lafayette, Louisiana
SUBJECT(S): Science DATE: April 16, 2002			TIME: 3 weeks

OBJECTIVE(S):	INTELLIGENCES:	TECHNOLOGIES:	NETS FOR STUDENTS:
■ To learn the basic anatomy of the brain, including the cerebrum, cerebellum, and brain stem; the left and right hemispheres; and the lobes of the brain.	Verbal Logical Visual Kinesthetic Naturalist	PowerPoint Inspiration Browser	3 Students use productivity tools to collaborate in constructing technology-enhanced models.
■ To explore the structure and function of neurons.	Logical Naturalist		

MATERIALS:	INTELLIGENCES:
Overhead Computer PowerPoint	Visual Kinesthetic Verbal/Visual
Inspiration	Verbal/Visual Naturalist
Web browser	Verbal/Visual

PROCEDURE:	INTELLIGENCES:
Prelesson:	
Read class text entitled *The Nervous System* (Glencoe Science).	Visual
Present PowerPoint slideshow highlighting key facts of brain structure.	Verbal
Have students explore hands-on Web sites through a teacher-created hotlist (www.kn.pacbell.com/wired/fil/pages/listthebraida.html).	Visual Verbal Kinesthetic
Lesson:	
Present overheads depicting neurons and illustrating transmission for review of concepts.	Visual Verbal
Use simple hand gestures to illustrate the components of the neuron. Have students imitate the following instructions:	Kinesthetic

TABLE 22 ■ "OUR BRAIN—THE 3-POUND WONDER" LESSON	
PROCEDURE:	**INTELLIGENCES:**
"Hold out your arm and spread your fingers. Your hand represents the 'cell body' (also called the 'soma'); your fingers represent 'dendrites' bringing information to the cell body; your arm represents the 'axon' taking information away from the cell body."	
(From *Neuroscience for Kids, Modeling the Nervous System, Simple Neuron Model,* http://faculty.washington.edu/chudler/chmodel.html)	
Conduct "Connect the Dots," an activity to simulate the number of neuronal connections:	Logical
"This exercise is to illustrate the complexity of the connections of the brain. Draw 10 dots on one side of a piece of paper and 10 dots on the other side of the paper. Assume these dots represent neurons, and assume that each neuron makes connections with the 10 dots on the other side of the paper. Then connect each dot on one side with the 10 dots on the other side. Remember that this is quite a simplification. Each neuron (dot) may actually make thousands of connections with other neurons. If you tried this your paper would be really messy!"	
(From *Neuroscience for Kids, Modeling the Nervous System. Connect the Dots,* http://faculty.washington.edu/chudler/chmodel.html)	
Use the outside game "Synaptic Tag" to follow up on the concept of how neurotransmitters cross the synapse to reach the dendrite:	Kinesthetic
"In the game of 'synaptic tag,' you are part of the synapse. The object of the game is to get as many neurotransmitters across the synapse to the dendrite without being caught (deactivated) by the enzyme. It is like a game of tag. Draw or find a space for the axon and a dendrite (see the picture below). Some players are neurotransmitters and they wait in the axon; other players are enzymes, they wait in the gap between the axon and the dendrite. It is best to have more neurotransmitters than enzymes. The enzymes are 'it.'"	
"When someone says 'go,' the neurotransmitters run across the synapse as fast as possible without being touched by an enzyme. If a neurotransmitter is touched by an enzyme, it must go back (be reabsorbed) into the axon and wait until the next turn. If a player makes it to the dendrite, the player is safe. Play as many times as you like. Make sure everyone has a chance to be a neurotransmitter and an enzyme."	

TABLE 22 ■ "OUR BRAIN—THE 3-POUND WONDER" LESSON	
PROCEDURE:	**INTELLIGENCES:**
(From *Neuroscience for Kids, Outside Games, Synaptic Tag,* http://faculty.washington.edu/chudler/outside.html)	
Lobes of the Brain: Present overheads depicting lobes of the brain for review of concepts.	
Have students work in small groups to create a model of the brain that simulates the brain in weight and consistency. Conduct the "Potato Head" activity:	Visual Verbal
"This activity is meant to simulate the actual weight and size of a human brain. ■ 5 cups instant potato flakes ■ 2.5 cups hot water ■ 2 cups sand Combine all ingredients in the Ziploc bag and mix. It should weigh about 3 pounds and simulate the texture of a human brain."	Kinesthetic Interpersonal
(From *Neuroscience for Kids, Modeling the Nervous System, Model a Brain,* http://faculty.washington.edu/chudler/chmodel.html)	
Given song selections as examples, the students will create a new song or jingle about a concept they have learned.	Verbal Musical
(From *Journey Into the Brain, Brainy Tunes,* www.morphonix. com/software/education/science/brain/game/songs/brainy_tunes. html)	
Postlesson:	
Create a "brain" display and invite younger students to view the projects created. Pair students and allow them to "teach" the concepts to the younger students. The display should include student-created material, opportunities for exploring brain models, and other interactive materials.	
ASSESSMENT:	**INTELLIGENCES:**
Working in pairs, the students will complete at least two projects:	
■ Create a model of the brain using any selected medium (clay, playdough, papier-mâché). The brain should be constructed according to scale and clearly depict the four lobes of the brain. Create a model of a neuron. It should include the axon, dendrites, and cell body.	Kinesthetic Logical Naturalist
■ Make a recording of at least five brain songs (original or ones reviewed in class).	Musical

TABLE 22 ■ "OUR BRAIN—THE 3-POUND WONDER" LESSON	
PROCEDURE:	**INTELLIGENCES:**
■ Create three illustrations of the brain: (1) show the four lobes of the brain, (2) show the left and right hemispheres, (3) show the cerebrum, cerebellum, and brain stem.	Visual Naturalist
■ Using simplified terminology, create a simple diagram of the lobes of the brain and their function to be presented to a class of third-grade students. Be prepared to be the teacher and teach your minilesson.	Visual Interpersonal Naturalist

How do we know when we have finally arrived as a technoconstructivist? It's a subjective judgment to some degree. I would argue that we never truly arrive; we simply keep working to evolve our instructional practices to more closely approximate the ideal. In short, I continue to aspire to be a technoconstructivist!

Reflections

1 Where would you place yourself in Noon's model of teacher technology use?

2 How can you accommodate the intelligences through technology as a technotraditionalist? What limits or assists this?

3 What kind of support do you need to become a technoconstructivist?

Chapter 9

Internet-Based Instruction

Perhaps the most promising of all the digital technologies is the Internet. Whereas operating systems evolve in perpetuity and software always offers something new and improved, the Internet operates free of any particular computer platform or private commercial interest. Within a connected classroom are all the resources and possibilities of the Internet, limited only by the vision of the teacher who implements its use. By the Internet, I am referring to a variety of technologies listed in Table 23.

The Internet is more than just Web sites. It is an interconnected virtual community of all kinds of multimedia information, interaction, and collaboration. By its very nature, the Internet is the most robust medium for addressing all the intelligences. It supports them seamlessly, in consort with and at each individual's ability level. Because it has a sophisticated structure, let's take a closer look at the components of the Internet before discussing its instructional implications.

There are two kinds of online collaboration, asynchronous (independent of time constraints) and synchronous (time dependent or conducted in real time).

Asynchronous Communication

Asynchronous forms of online communication include electronic mail, mailing lists, and message boards. Asynchronous communication affords the user the luxury of posting and responding to messages at any time from any location that has an Internet connection. It is popular because it allows users to interact free of time constraints. You don't have to be online at 7 p.m. on a Thursday night in order to meet with your peers. New messages will be there for you to find whenever you have the time to check. You can check your e-mail or log in to a newsgroup at any hour on any day of the week and catch up on the most recent messages your colleagues have posted. Asynchronous communication can be used in instruction in the following ways.

Electronic Mail

Students in many classes have used e-mail to correspond with students from other parts of the world as "keypals" (penpals via the keyboard). Teachers correspond with one another to plan writing tasks between the classes. The evolving relationship can include sharing picture files as e-mail attachments, digital video greetings, and packages of materials sent by "snail" mail. When classes are within close proximity, an end-of-year trip to visit the other class is also a popular practice. There are a number of online services, including ePals (www.epals.com/), Gaggle (www.gaggle.net/), and the Keypals Club (www.teaching.com/keypals/), that will help screen prospective classes for you to keypal with.

E-mail projects are also popular among connected classrooms. Remember the Great Mail Race Project of the early 1990s when classes snail-mailed letters to "Any School" c/o a random ZIP code in every state? They waited to hear back from all 50 states and charted the responses they received in the classroom. In today's classrooms, students conduct a modified version of this project using e-mail, sending out electronic mailings to schools around the country or even around the world. The resulting interaction among classes promotes language arts, social

Table 23

Internet Technologies

TECHNOLOGY	INTELLIGENCES
ELECTRONIC MAIL (E-MAIL)	Verbal Interpersonal
MAILING LISTS	Verbal Logical Interpersonal
MESSAGE BOARDS	Verbal Logical Interpersonal Naturalist
CHAT	Verbal Visual Interpersonal Naturalist Existential
MULTIUSER VIRTUAL ENVIRONMENTS (MUVE)	Verbal Logical Visual Kinesthetic Interpersonal Intrapersonal Naturalist Existential
WORLD WIDE WEB (WWW)	Verbal Logical Visual Musical Kinesthetic Interpersonal Intrapersonal Naturalist Existential

studies, mathematics, science, and even health. Cooperating teachers can plan topics for students to write on, projects in which data can be shared, exchanges of information about communities and countries, and much, much more.

The Flat Stanley Project (www.enoreo.on.ca/flatstanley/index.htm) is another example of a snail-mail phenomenon that has taken on a new online life. Based on a character in a book by Jeff Brown, Flat Stanley is a boy who is flattened by a billboard so completely that he is able to travel by being folded and mailed. Students contact fellow Internet travelers from around the world to send them a replica of Flat Stanley. Recipients of a Flat Stanley take him along on their daily tasks and keep a record of their adventures together. They then send a recounting of Stanley's visit back to the class from which Stanley came. Now, however, it can all be done online using e-mail and a digital camera. Think of the money a class saves just on postage!

Ask-an-expert services are another great way to use e-mail. Consider studying the solar system and having your students e-mail a NASA scientist when they have a question they can't find an answer to in the resources available at school, or e-mail a U.S. Geological Survey geologist when they want to learn more about plate tectonics. Ask-an-expert services allow you to do just that. They are typically free of charge but often require a week or two before you get a response. However, the result is worth the wait when your classroom comes alive with the response from an actual expert in the area your class is studying. To find out more about these services, simply go to your favorite search engine and conduct a search on "ask an expert." You'll be amazed at the results you find!

E-mail projects tend to promote the verbal and interpersonal intelligences most prominently. They rely on a class's commitment to stay in touch and respond on a regular basis, so teachers and students who are "people people" and find writing a pleasant, easy task will enjoy participating in them. E-mail projects are also an excellent way to promote the verbal and interpersonal intelligences in students who may need to more fully develop these paths to learning. The one caveat for teachers is that e-mail projects require a lot of monitoring. You will want to conference with your students and know their status in the project. Furthermore, if you have a strict acceptable use policy (AUP), you will need to screen correspondence. Be sure you know your school's AUP!

Mailing Lists

Mailing lists can be very useful in conducting classroom projects. While it is not necessarily a project unto itself, a well-constructed mailing list can augment a project by creating a virtual online community. For example, if you are collaborating with other classes online, adding all the students' e-mail addresses to a mailing list allows anyone on the list to send out one e-mail that is automatically delivered to everyone on the list. This can be very handy when making an announcement, posing a general question, or sharing information.

A mailing list like this is set up by having one common e-mail address for the list to which everyone can send announcements. When an e-mail is sent to that address, it is then distributed to everyone. For a project mailing list, it is best to have a moderator who screens all mailings sent to the list's e-mail address before the messages are posted. This helps keep the list free of off-topic discussions and misinformation. The moderator also can add members to or delete members from the mailing list, keeping it a safe, private community. Most important, mailing lists are password protected, so you can maintain a closed community without stray visitors having access to your archives.

Mailing lists tend to stimulate the verbal, interpersonal, and existential intelligences. Their communal nature really helps students feel that they are part of something bigger, and the lists are still largely a haven for those who like to write and interact. Nonetheless, mailing lists also have a business-like function as members keep one another informed and up to date on project happenings.

Consider the technology coordinators' mailing list moderated by Tim Landeck of Santa Cruz, California. This list is an asynchronous forum for instructional technology coordinators, who can pose questions, generate possible solutions, and share experiences common to the group. When a member posts a question about how to set up a mail server for his or her school, the question is sent out to everyone on the list. Colleagues can then respond by e-mail with their recommendations, which are also distributed to everyone on the list. If the problem is cut-and-dried—for example, how to set up a mail server—the list may see a small flourish of activity on the topic and then quiet down again.

However, when a more controversial topic comes up—for example, the use of filtering software—the activity level on the list may increase sharply as e-mails are posted to the list in response to different points of view. Regardless of the topic, a sense of belonging and commitment to the group develops over time. Members of the list belong to a community they can access any time or any day (existential). They can brainstorm ideas (visual) and solve problems (logical) while getting to know one another as online friends (interpersonal). Moreover, because this list is specifically for technology coordinators, there is a common set of values and concerns shared on the list (intrapersonal). It is truly a cyber support group.

Message Boards

Message boards can include discussion groups, newsgroups, and even archived mailing lists. An e-mail message comes directly to you, but a message board is housed at a fixed Internet address that you must visit in order to participate. Some message board services will notify you by e-mail when new messages have been posted, but you still have to log in to the virtual location in order to read and respond.

The dynamic of a message board is that interaction takes place within a finite set of participants, so a virtual community is built over time. Not everyone has to agree or get along, but over time they all get to know one another well through their exchanges. Furthermore, as it evolves each message board community cultivates its own culture, which includes a recorded history, an inside humor, and expressions and shorthand unique to that group.

Moreover, message boards are archived at their virtual location. You can go back and look through a certain topic or "thread" that was discussed and read from its initial posting on the board through its conclusion. The metaphor of a thread serves message boards well because each individual thread on a board is woven into the fabric that becomes the community identified with it. Because of this archiving feature, message boards not only serve the verbal, interpersonal, and existential intelligences, they also accommodate the naturalist intelligence well. Message board archives provide a structure and organization that allow the naturalist learner in all of us to make sense of digital, text-based communication.

The Teacher to Teacher (T2T) community has changed from mailing lists to message boards for just these reasons. Now when you subscribe to this service, instead of getting several daily mailings (verbal) you can simply log in to the site and participate on the boards that address your professional interests (intrapersonal). Threads develop and evolve as the group sees the need to pursue pertinent topics (interpersonal), and the sense of community at T2T is very tangible—even to a first-time visitor (existential).

Because the message board is asynchronous, you can log in at any time of the day, or go for weeks without checking in and then catch up all at once (musical). The true mark of a community in a message board is that once you participate in a message board of particular interest to you, it is very difficult to stop participating or remove yourself completely from the board. The feeling of belonging keeps you coming back!

Synchronous Communication

Synchronous communication includes real-time chat and multiuser virtual environments (MUVEs). The distinguishing mark of synchronous communication is that it takes place in real time. In other words, when you post a message, it is read at the exact moment it is posted. You can then read responses from others within seconds of posting your own message.

This is a text-based version of face-to-face conversation; it is spontaneous, fast-paced, and dynamic. While asynchronous forms of communication seem passive by nature, synchronous interaction is active and engaging. It requires that the parties involved be online at the same moment regardless of their location or time zone in order to communicate with each other in a text-based environment.

Chat

There are a number of ways to chat online, including Web-based chat, Internet relay chat, and instant messaging chat. Web-based chat is extremely common nowadays because JAVA applets have made it very easy to offer chat on a Web page. This phenomenon has become commonplace enough that these chats are free, usually only requiring you to register for security purposes. Web-based chat is typically social in nature; participants come and go without necessarily feeling a sense of belonging. Usually a core group of familiar users faithfully return to a specific Web site chat, but they are outnumbered by the number of visitors who come to see what the chat is all about and then move on. Even the more sophisticated Web site chats that propose themes of common interest tend to have a low rate of success in building a large core of repeat users. A community is hard to build this way.

Internet relay chat (IRC) requires the installation of software that helps you connect to the Internet and then use a custom-designed chat interface. The software is usually free, and so is the chat. After you have set up the software on your system, you simply log in and set up your personal profile. You can then access thousands of chats by topic, bookmark those chat "rooms" you wish to return to, and even create your own room if you desire.

Unlike Web-based chats, IRC tends to build strong core groups of participants that resemble minicommunities. What is unique is that these core groups are not necessarily tied to one chat room; instead, they can move among rooms according to their whim and still remain an identifiable group. The culture created through IRC has very few boundaries, so you will come across every kind of topic imaginable among the chat rooms in IRC. This makes it an inappropriate environment for children.

More familiar to the general public are the chat services provided by national Internet Service Providers (ISPs) like CompuServe, Microsoft Network, and America Online. (Did you know America Online started out as a message board?) These services also require you to install software, and there is a monthly subscriber fee and terms of service that set boundaries on what topics and behavior are allowed in the chat areas. Like IRC, there is a variety of chat rooms available and users can create their own if they wish, but the rooms do not number in the thousands and the topics conform to the more generally held mores and conventions of society at large. Again, some core members are often referred to as "regulars" in these ISP chats, but the bulk of a chat room's traffic consists of transient visitors just looking to see what is happening.

The most popular recent chat tools are instant messaging applications. They are commonly free and include such names as ICQ, Instant Messenger, and Yahoo Messenger. These tools connect to the Internet whenever you do and let you know when friends are online. You can send messages back and forth privately without having to log in to a chat room, and you can even record and save your messages.

Moreover, you can conduct an instant message chat while working in other applications because the chat interface is a small window that does not block your view of other programs you have running. There's a nice sense of control with instant messaging because you can offer your username exclusively to those people you want to be able to contact you, and you can block access of users from whom you do not want to hear. There is a very low incidence of transient traffic interrupting your private chats. Also, you can chat as a group using instant messaging, so the notion of having to be tied down to a virtual chat room is being made obsolete.

Like asynchronous communication, synchronous chat is a text-based function that is limited in what it can offer the user. You can interact in real time. In some cases you can exchange files. But the potential for more than the interaction of ideas in a social forum is limited.

Synchronous interaction often has the effect of lowering people's inhibitions, allowing them to act out in ways they would never behave face to face. In fact, because of the benefits chat offers it has carved an online niche for itself where it is seen as a tool for fun and exploration. More sophisticated MUVE users are easily insulted when MUVEs are referred to as "chat rooms." Yet, log in to any chat community and note the high level of activity and the volume of people using the service. Chat is the offbeat cousin no one likes to mention in the family of synchronous communication.

The verbal, interpersonal, and existential intelligences are easily stimulated by synchronous chat. To use a chat environment for more than this, you would need to have a task-oriented group of people using the interface for a specific goal. For example, if you have a group of teachers from geographically remote locations meet on IRC to critique and recommend software applications for a conference presentation they are planning, they would quickly use their logical and intrapersonal intelligences as well. It always comes back to the context in which the application is used. The context dictates the intelligences.

MUVEs

If chats are the lowbrow version of synchronous communication, MUVEs are the highbrow. In a MUVE you can communicate in text in real time, move throughout virtual places, create your own virtual persona, and work collaboratively to complete tasks.

A large part of a MUVE is the metaphor used to create this virtual world. A MUVE can use the metaphor of a college campus, a castle, an amusement park, or any other environment familiar to us in the real world. In entering a MUVE, you immerse yourself in its metaphor and learn to function accordingly. You create a persona that will be accepted there.

For example, in a castle metaphor you would want to create a persona—a knight, prince, lady, or duchess—that is consistent with a castle's theme. You can create or select an image that represents you in the MUVE so that people will recognize you, and that persona will help define your place in this virtual world.

A good example of a MUVE is TappedIn (TI) (http://tappedin.org), which is designed as a virtual world for educators. Its metaphor is an office tower with adjacent buildings in which you can have your own office space and participate in public areas of the MUVE. When you first enter TI, you are welcomed at the help desk. You can make your way quickly to an office or the auditorium if you are there for a scheduled event, or you can leisurely meet colleagues as you move from room to room. You can only "see" colleagues who are in the same "room" that you are in, although you can find others through various the functions TI offers.

Because it is designed for professional educators, TI has a number of affordances that promote interaction and collaboration. Participants can store and save files, use a "tape recorder" that will record discussions and archive them for future reference, create "notes" they can call up on command to explain ideas to others, and even participate in project Web sites that everyone in the room can see and discuss together. As a MUVE, TI addresses a number of intelligences:

- **VERBAL**—text-based communication

- **LOGICAL**—file storage, scheduled events, structured environment

- **VISUAL**—navigating through virtual rooms, sharing Web sites

- **INTERPERSONAL**—collaboration with colleagues

- **NATURALIST**—community hierarchy and classification of archived files

- **EXISTENTIAL**—belonging to a virtual community

TI also has a Student Activity Center that allows teachers to bring in their classes to work online in a safe, controlled environment. Teachers create student IDs under their own TI username, and students don't have access to any other part of TI except the Activity Center.

Several years ago my fourth graders were the first class to use the Activity Center in TI. We were collaborating with seventh graders at a middle school 90 minutes north of us in Virginia to research Thomas Jefferson and create a Web site presenting his accomplishments. Because of the physical distance between the two schools, we could not collaborate face to face. Because of the visual nature of the project, e-mail and chat were of only limited use to the students. TappedIn offered a solution to our needs.

We were able to meet in the Student Activity Center in six small groups because there were six small studios within the Activity Center. I created six tape recorders and placed one in each studio so that each work session was recorded while my counterpart and I moved from studio to studio to spot check group work and help out where needed. At the end of the session all tape-recorded transcripts were automatically e-mailed directly to me so that they could be distributed to the groups as they continued working separately.

The project came together well. We knew it was a success after students began putting together whole pages on Jefferson's childhood, education, inventions, accomplishments, and presidency. You can see the final product at http://surfaquarium.com/tj.htm. We capped off the project and the school year by meeting at Camden Yards in June to watch an Orioles' game together and finally put names and faces together after all our online work! MUVEs are a wonderful way to promote a variety of intelligences online.

Collaborative Projects

Collaborative projects offer the possibility of developing students' higher order thinking skills and accommodating all the intelligences by combining online and offline resources to make for truly memorable learning.

Collaborative projects can take many forms, as evidenced by my list of projects at the Surfaquarium (http://surfaquairum.com/projects.htm). Collaborative projects are multidisciplinary and multi-intelligence. They can be:

- classroom centered
- Web based
- challenge based
- contest based
- task-oriented
- data driven
- time sensitive
- ongoing
- asynchronous
- synchronous

Collaborative projects are typically designed by teachers who are looking for like-minded colleagues to join their classes and complete a project together. After a teacher has designed a project, he or she announces it through teacher mailing lists and project archives like Global Schoolhouse (GSH) (www.lightspan.com/common/pages/linkout5.asp?loc=gsh.lightspan.com/pr/index.cfm?&setInternal=true&_prod=GSH). This helps recruit other classes to the project.

Several specific elements should be part of the design of any online project.

- **GOAL**—state the purpose of the project up front so interested teachers will know what the project entails.

- **TIMELINE**—give the specific dates for registration and each subsequent stage of the project so teachers will know how it is paced.

- **RESOURCES**—name specific resources the teacher will need to have access to in order to participate: Internet connection, hardware, software, hands-on materials, texts, and so forth.

- **FINAL PRODUCT**—describe the final product participating classes will create in the project.

- **PROJECT WEB SITE**—create a Web site that participating classes can visit at any time to go over project information and announcements and share ideas and final products.

- **CONTACT PERSON**—provide an e-mail address where the sponsoring teacher can be reached at any time.

To maximize your collaborative project for MI, you will want to follow these steps:

1. Create the outline for the project.

2. Identify the intelligences stimulated by the project tasks you have outlined.

3. Edit and revise your outline to accommodate all the intended intelligences.

A Collaborative Unit Template

Table 24 provides a template for creating a collaborative unit. (The CD-ROM accompanying this book also contains the template in the MI_Templates file.)

Note how each task is identified with a specific intelligence or intelligences that allow for easy identification and planning. Note also that the technologies used are mapped from each task through each intelligence. Much like a well-designed lesson, a well-designed project should never have its technologies selected until you have first identified the tasks and intelligences you intend to employ.

Consider the eIditarod Project (http://surfaquarium.com/e_iditarod.htm) I sponsored in winter 2001. Classes were invited to follow and study the Iditarod Sled Dog Race in March by using online resources, following a musher of their choice, and writing to the musher at the end of the race. In one high-interest collection of activities, the project brought together the required study of animals (the sled dogs), weather, geography, mapping, elapsed time, letter writing, and the use of the Web, e-mail, and problem solving. The project entailed much more than that, though, as evidenced by the plan outlined in Table 25. (Table 25 appears at the end of this chapter).

Note how the unit stimulates all nine of the intelligences throughout the course of the project. Problem-solving tasks e-mailed to classes during the race included determining ways to get additional snow on the trail where it had melted due to unusually warm temperatures, plans for spacing out required rest stops on the trail so a dog team had the best chance to win, suggestions for the number of dogs to use during different phases of the race to maximize sled speed, designing and building dog sleds using craft sticks, making Inuit carvings out of soap, and building igloos out of sugar cubes.

Approximately 125 classes from around the country signed up for the project, with lots of active participation and interaction. By visiting the project Web site, you can see student work and the final letters to mushers. Because it involved a high-interest topic and all the intelligences, it was a successful project for everyone involved. Have an idea for a great collaborative project? Plug it into the template and you'll be well on your way to success.

There is no more effective way to empower teachers to use the Internet than to give them the tools to be successful. One teacher, Marge Shasberger, did just that by creating a unit that introduced the wealth of the Internet to her colleagues. She modified the MI Collaborative Unit Template to create a staff development project for her fellow teachers. It involved all the intelligences and required the use of a variety of technologies. Table 26 summarizes the project. (Table 26 appears at the end of this chapter).

Table 24

Multiple Intelligences Collaborative Unit Template

TITLE:			
GRADE LEVEL:			
OBJECTIVE(S)			
TIMELINE (WITH SPECIFIC DUE DATES):			
RESOURCES:			

TASKS:	INTELLIGENCES:	TECHNOLOGIES:	NETS FOR STUDENTS:

FINAL PRODUCT:		INTELLIGENCES:

ASSESSMENT:		INTELLIGENCES:

Ms. Shasberger involves a combination of intelligences and technologies to create a powerful set of learning experiences for teachers. By using these different Internet-based technologies, they will be ready to work and learn online with their students. Also note that Ms. Shasberger includes the use of the intelligences in her assessment rubric of the students' final projects. MI can be a body of knowledge for students to master as well as a process they see within themselves!

Reflections

1 What forms of synchronous and asynchronous communication would work well with your learners and curriculum?

2 What topics in your curriculum are ripe for developing a Web-based project?

3 Classify the eIditarod project according to Noon's model and explain the rationale behind your decision.

Table 25
"The eIditarod" Collaborative Unit

TITLE: The eIditarod	
GRADE LEVEL: 7–8	
OBJECTIVE(S): To follow a musher through the Iditarod Sled Dog Race and write to the musher at the conclusion of the race.	
TIMELINE (WITH SPECIFIC DUE DATES): 5 days (1 week)	

RESOURCES:

January 8–26	Open registration period
January 29–February 9	Create a wall map of the trail
February 11–23	Select a musher to follow in the race
February 26–March 2	Study and prepare for the big event
March 3–end of race	Follow your musher and send an e-mail to each checkpoint
March 31	Post your final written task to the project Web site

TASKS:	INTELLIGENCES:	TECHNOLOGIES:	NETS FOR STUDENTS:
1. Study the trail's geography and read musher biographies.	Verbal Logical Naturalist	Web site	1. Basic operations and concepts 2. Social, ethical, and human issues
2. Create a wall-sized map of the trail using a grid and a compass rose.	Visual Logical Kinesthetic Naturalist	Printer Paper Paints	3. Technology productivity tools 4. Technology communications tools
3. Select a musher to follow in the race	Intrapersonal	Web site	5. Technology research tools
4. Track on the wall map the selected musher's progress and weather conditions during the race.	Logical Musical Existential	Web site	6. Technology problem-solving and decision-making tools

TABLE 25 ■ "THE EIDIATROD" COLLABORATIVE UNIT

TASKS:	INTELLIGENCES:	TECHNOLOGIES:	NETS FOR STUDENTS:
5. Send an e-mail to each checkpoint the selected musher reaches on the trail.	Verbal Interpersonal	E-mail	
6. Receive a response from us here at the project each time you write.	Verbal Interpersonal	E-mail	
7. With support from your classroom teacher, complete the problem-solving tasks we send you by e-mail.	Logical Interpersonal Musical Naturalist	Hands-on materials	
8. Arrive in Nome vicariously with your selected musher.	Logical Existential	Web site	
9. Submit a letter to your musher for publication on the project Web site.	Verbal Intrapersonal Existential	E-mail Web site	

FINAL PRODUCT:	INTELLIGENCES:
Publish a letter to the musher you have followed sharing your new knowledge and experiences in following the race	Verbal Interpersonal Intrapersonal Existential

ASSESSMENT:	INTELLIGENCES:
All letters submitted by participating teachers will be accepted for publication as long as they are free of errors and have appropriate content. Letters will demonstrate what the students learned from following the race. The letters will be published on the Web site and sent to the mushers to whom they were written.	Verbal Interpersonal Intrapersonal Existential

Table 26

"Teachers on the Web" Collaborative Unit

TITLE: Teachers on the Web	TEACHER: Marge Shasberger
	Placer County Office of Education
SUBJECT(S): Staff Development	Auburn, California

TIMELINE (WITH SPECIFIC DUE DATES): 5 days (1 week)

OBJECTIVE(S):	INTELLIGENCES:	TECHNOLOGIES:	PROPOSED CALIFORNIA PERFORMANCE STANDARDS FOR EDUCATORS— TECHNOLOGY (http://ctap.k12.ca. us/grants/teachstds. html)
To be able to use the Internet as a viable resource in the classroom. The teacher will demonstrate an understanding of how to use this electronic tool as an educational tool by:			
■ Indicating an understanding of search techniques, how to access major resource sites on the Internet, and the proper use and documentation of cyber information.	Verbal Logical Visual Naturalist Existential	Browser	Level One— Personal Proficiency A. Performance Standards 1, 2, 3, 5, 6
■ Understanding the use of e-mail, listservs, and bulletin boards for communication by students in their classrooms with other students or experts in a field, and for their own professional growth through communications	Verbal Logical Visual Interpersonal Intrapersonal Naturalist Existential	Browser Mail client	Level Two— Instructional Proficiency A. Performance Standards 1, 2, 3, 5 B. Initial Assessment A-4

TABLE 26 ■ "TEACHERS ON THE WEB" COLLABORATIVE UNIT

TASKS:	INTELLIGENCES:	TECHNOLOGIES:	PROPOSED CPSE:
with other teachers as a support/ informational group.			Level Three— Mentor Proficiency A. Performance Standards 1, 2, 3, 4, 5
■ Explaining the possibilities avail-able to students for various forms of presentations and expression of ideas and concepts learned in a lesson.	Verbal Logical Visual Musical Kinesthetic Interpersonal Intrapersonal Naturalist Existential	Presentation software, multimedia software, text and graphics software	Level Four— Leadership Proficiency A. Performance Expectations 1, 2

RESOURCES:	INTELLIGENCES:
Hardware:	
Computers	Kinesthetic
Printers	Visual
Projection equipment	Visual
Digital camera	Visual
Camcorders	Visual/Verbal
Software:	
Browser	Verbal, Visual, Interpersonal, Existential
Mail client	Verbal, Visual, Interpersonal, Existential
Presentation software	Verbal, Visual, Musical, Kinesthetic
Multimedia software	Verbal, Visual, Musical, Kinesthetic
Text and graphics software	Verbal, Visual
Other Materials:	
Hotlists for resource sites	Verbal, Logical, Naturalist, Existential
Art supplies	Visual, Kinesthetic

DAILY TASKS:	INTELLIGENCES:
Prelesson Class Preparation: This will include the preparation of sample scavenger hunts, hotlists, rules for using the Internet (searching techniques, using e-mail, downloading materials, citing sources, and so forth), preparation of sample rubrics for evaluating Web sites and classroom projects, sample lesson outlines, and sample lessons.	

TABLE 26 ■ "TEACHERS ON THE WEB" COLLABORATIVE UNIT	
DAILY TASKS:	**INTELLIGENCES:**
Day 1–Introduction to the Internet and the World Wide Web	
Hour 1: Overview of class activities and expectations and introductions. The class will take the MI survey.	Logical Intrapersonal
Hours 2-4: Introduction to the Internet and the World Wide Web.	
Brief history and explanation of the Internet and the World Wide Web.	Verbal
Discussion of basic terms and tools for using the World Wide Web, including the use of and similarities and differences among search engines, directories, and other tools.	Verbal Interpersonal
ACTIVITY—Students will practice ways to search effectively, using prepared subject sheets and visiting search sites.	Verbal Logical
ACTIVITY—Students will visit various informational sites that give instructions on searching, e.g., Kathy Schrock's site (www.capecod.net/schrockguide/yp/iypsrch.htm), the Computer Strategies site (www.compstrategies.com/resources/search.html), and the Eureka site (www.gocee.com/eureka/eureka_i.htm).	Verbal Logical
Demonstration of basic classroom applications, including scavenger hunts, research hotlists, independent searches for information, and proper preparation of activities for classroom use. The class will discuss ethical and legal issues involved in using the Internet and the World Wide Web as a resource and informational tool.	Verbal Intrapersonal
ACTIVITY—Students will complete a sample scavenger hunt prepared by the teacher, then choose a subject of interest, and then prepare a scavenger hunt of their own using their own search procedures. Students will explore various teacher resource sites, including Education World (www.education-world.com), Computer Strategies (www.compstrategies.com/resources/k12edsites.html), Dewpoint (http://ivory.lm.com/~mundie/DDHC/DDH.htm), Global School Network (www.gsn.org/wce), and the George Lucas Foundation (www.glef.org).	Logical Visual
Hours 5-6: Using e-mail, listservs, and other communication sources such as bulletin boards, the class will review the various methods of participating in dialogues with other users.	Verbal Existential
ACTIVITY 1—The class will e-mail messages to each other.	Verbal Interpersonal
ACTIVITY 2—The class will explore the listservs available on Lizst, the mailing list directory (http://www.liszt.com), and Education World (www.education-world.com). Students will subscribe to at least one location of their choice.	Logical Intrapersonal

TABLE 26 ■ "TEACHERS ON THE WEB" COLLABORATIVE UNIT	
	INTELLIGENCES:
ACTIVITY 3—The class will explore the Scholastic Web site, locating an active bulletin board of their choice for discussion.	Verbal Intrapersonal
ACTIVITY 4—The class will explore e-mail and project Web sites for classroom participation, e.g., Classroom Connect (www.classroom.com/home.asp).	Logical Intrapersonal Existential
Day 2—Presentation Software *Hours 1-3:* The class will review the basic tools and procedures used to effectively prepare a PowerPoint presentation.	
ACTIVITY 1—Using prepared slide presentations, students will practice modifying a slideshow by changing text, adding a slide, importing graphics, and becoming familiar with PowerPoint template slides, design templates, and presentation templates.	Logical Kinesthetic
ACTIVITY 2—Using the Outline View, students will prepare an outline of their lives. This will include such main topics as the individual's history, personal information (likes, dislikes, place of residence, family makeup), educational background, teaching experience, and goals for this class.	Verbal Logical Visual Musical Kinesthetic
Hours 4-6: The class will explore advanced techniques, including slide transitions, animation, backgrounds, and importing outside resources (e.g., graphics and text from sources such as Word, the Internet, and digital cameras).	
ACTIVITY 1—The class will explore slide effects using a prepared slideshow.	Visual
ACTIVITY 2—The class will apply slide effects to individual information outlines.	Visual
ACTIVITY 3—The class will present slideshows.	Verbal Visual Musical
Day 3—The class will be divided as evenly as possible into groups made up of different intelligences. Assignments will include the preparation of a lesson in a subject area of the group's choice for use in a classroom.	

TABLE 26 ■ "TEACHERS ON THE WEB" COLLABORATIVE UNIT	
DAILY TASKS:	**INTELLIGENCES:**
Hours 1-3—Groups will be formed. Each group will choose the subject or theme for the lesson to be presented to the class. The group will establish an objective for the lesson, decide on the method of presenting the lesson to the class, and determine the types of resources to be used (searches, project sites, e-mail sites, and so forth).	Verbal Logical Interpersonal Intrapersonal
Hours 4-6—At the beginning of the afternoon session, each group will be asked to outline the basic idea it has decided to work on, including the assignment each group member will focus on. Each group will indicate how it intends to use the technology as a tool in the lesson it is preparing. The remainder of the afternoon will be spent preparing the group activity.	Verbal Naturalist
Day 4—Ongoing work on projects	
Hours 1-3—Group activities related to the project.	Verbal Interpersonal
Hours 4-6—Using the class as a sample student population, groups will begin to finalize their class presentations and activities to demonstrate how technology will be used in their lessons.	Intrapersonal Interpersonal
Day 5—Class Presentation	
Groups will present their individual class projects, including activities in which students would be required to participate if the lesson were offered in a school environment.	Verbal Visual Musical
Groups will assess their peer presenters, offering feedback and suggestions.	Intrapersonal Interpersonal

TABLE 26 ■ "TEACHERS ON THE WEB" COLLABORATIVE UNIT	
ASSESSMENT:	**INTELLIGENCES:**
Rubric:	
Technology Tools:	Interpersonal
1. The group activity did not effectively employ tools to maximize the use of Internet as a classroom tool.	Logical Existential
2. The group demonstrated a basic understanding of the use of technology tools (search tools, e-mail, multimedia software)	
3. The group exhibited a clear understanding of the use of technology tools and the application of these tools to effectively navigate and use the Internet and its resources.	
Integration:	Verbal
1. The group did not establish legitimate use of the Internet as a required resource tool in the preparation of the final project.	Interpersonal Logical Existential
2. The group activity demonstrated a basic understanding of the Internet as a useful research tool.	
3. The group project relied on the use of the Internet as an essential tool for researching the subject or curricular area of the chosen lesson.	
Presentation:	Verbal
1. The final project was not presented through the use of technology media, nor did it depend on a technology component for the class presentation.	Visual Interpersonal Logical Musical
2. The group project used a minimum of one technology resource in its presentation.	Existential
3. The presentation to the class demonstrated the use of several different media tools to enhance the lesson and maximize interaction by the "students."	
Lesson:	Logical
1. The final lesson activity allowed for the optional use of technology in the classroom activities. The class was not involved in a presentation of the lesson.	Interpersonal Naturalist Existential
2. The use of technology as a resource for the lesson was encouraged, and a basic outline of the activities to further this use was included. Class participation was encouraged.	

TABLE 26 ■ "TEACHERS ON THE WEB" COLLABORATIVE UNIT	
DAILY TASKS:	**INTELLIGENCES:**
3. The final project included firm goals requiring the use of technology as an essential tool in the research, implementation, and presentation of the lesson objective. Class participation was ongoing and interactive. The class experimented with all aspects of the proposed lesson.	
Multiple Intelligences:	
1. The group activity demonstrated a single vision or presentation style.	Verbal Logical
2. The group activity showed the input of several different learning and teaching methods.	Visual Kinesthetic Musical
3. The group activity was presented to the class in several different ways, e.g., a well-thought-out research hotlist, an exciting slideshow presentation, and an artistic class handout, allowing the class to participate in different activities and demonstrating the input and skill of the various group members.	Interpersonal Intrapersonal Naturalist Existential

Chapter 10

Assessment

The hallmark of a great lesson, unit, or project is its results. Say what you will about the latest and greatest technology or the newest trend to come down the pike, master teachers know that it all is for naught if instruction doesn't lead to mastery of a learning objective. In fact, veteran teachers can be the hardest group to sell a new idea to, not because they are unwilling to expand on their repertoire of strategies but because they've seen so many bandwagons pass by their classroom never to be heard from again. If it is worthwhile and it works, it will find its way through their door. The proof is in the performance, and assessments measure performance.

What has been so remarkable about Howard Gardner's work from the beginning is that Gardner did not try to package MI theory to mass produce teaching kits for a profit, nor did he come to educators promising it would revolutionize the way they look at teaching and learning. Instead, educators approached Gardner, asking what the application of his theory could mean for schools. In his disarming, unassuming way, Gardner has responded that he leaves it up to the education professionals to answer those questions. After all, he reasons, they are the experts.

Using MI theory with learners has been a grassroots movement from its inception. Teachers have responded enthusiastically to the potential of this new model for instruction. Yet the ramifications go much further than we realize. Too many of us tout the legitimacy of Gardner's work and in the same breath ask if there is a prepackaged MI curriculum or a series of MI volumes containing reproducible activity sheets. We are missing the far-reaching implications of subscribing to Gardner's model. If multiple intelligences exist, then all bets are off on everything that has become so standardized about education. If multiple intelligences exist, then we need to find a new model for teaching and measuring student mastery.

Formative and Summative Assessments

Because learning is an ongoing process when addressing MI through technology, both formative and summative forms of assessment must take place. Formative assessments are snapshots in time that allow both the teacher and student to check on progress in learning. Formative assessments are ongoing and provide information that allows the teacher to modify instruction to increase opportunities for student success. For example, Mr. Houghton may have stated his objective as mastery of long division, but when he realizes students are still struggling with the two-digit multiplication algorithm, he revises his plans to revisit the process and strengthen their skills before proceeding with his original objective. In this way formative assessment and instruction form a continuous cycle that fuels itself. Figure 6 shows this cycle.

Figure 6. Cycle of Formative Assessment and Instruction

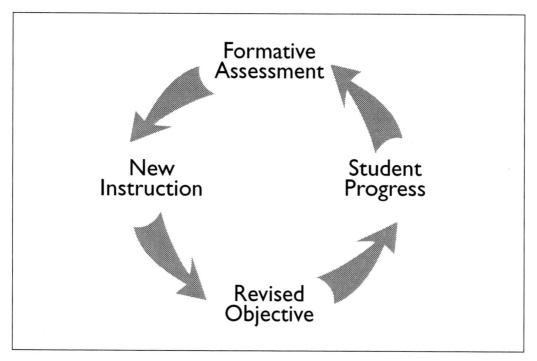

Summative assessments are measures of student success at the completion of a lesson or unit. They require students to take larger skills and concepts and apply them at higher levels of thinking. For this reason, traditional paper-and-pencil assessments have used essays, word problems, and lengthy objective sections to measure the degree to which students have truly mastered material. Traditionally, summative assessments have been very final in the way they have been implemented. Once the test on the Reconstruction was given before spring break, it was a hallmark for the school year that this chapter in history was over. What if those summative assessment scores were used to help determine the next unit of instruction, though? What if the summative assessment cycle was also used in planning for new instruction?

Summative assessment is an important piece of the teaching puzzle. If you intend to build on your instruction with new skills and content, it is vital to accurately measure what you've taught if you wish to know what students have actually mastered and to what degree they have mastered it. After all, if you haven't taught logarithms with a graphing calculator successfully, what's the point of moving on to quadratic equations? We all agree on that. The question becomes: How do we conduct our summative assessment? Are we using strictly paper-and-pencil assessments, and if so, why? We know that students with a strong kinesthetic or visual intelligence can master quadratic equations, but we also know that they will need to conceptualize and analyze them differently from those students possessing a strong logical intelligence. Is your classroom a sink-or-swim experience, or do your students all rise with the water level as they find their own effective ways to stay afloat?

Making Good Assessment Choices

Consider the role that assessment plays in a computer lab through the choices of two second-grade teachers who are both responsible for science standards on life cycles, metamorphosis, and animal migration.

Teacher A always makes sure she is in the lab for her allotted computer time. She quickly gets her students on the machines to draw and paint pictures of butterflies while she sits at an empty countertop grading papers. When the 45 minutes are up the kids can say they've had their computer time, and they love the idea of spending three-quarters of an hour drawing. This teacher had no interaction with her students, and she assumes that they will see the connection between their classroom study of butterfly migration and this unstructured lab time.

Teacher B also always makes sure she has her class in the computer lab on time. She uses the projector at the demonstration station to guide her class through a virtual tracking of Monarch butterflies migrating from the northeastern United States to Central America. All students are on task and following her lead as they discover the majesty of one of nature's most impressive annual treks. When students have questions or concerns, she is able to address them promptly, and before lab time is over she has each student working on a Monarch butterfly scavenger hunt she uploaded to the school Web site weeks before. As students work on their hunt she is free to move around the lab and interact with them as they apply what they know about the Monarch. Teacher B will use the results of each child's hunt to determine where she will go next in her science instruction for the next six weeks.

Which students understood the goal of their lab-based lesson? Which teacher addresses more intelligences in her classroom? Which teacher will have more success when it is time for the state standardized tests?

But someone may say, "What about those standardized tests? If I have my students learn cooperatively and complete all kinds of projects all year, they will never be ready for those state tests." The next time you hear that argument, remember my student Jamie and the incredible academic achievements he made in his fourth-grade year with less traditional instruction and assessment than he had ever experienced in the primary grades. Forcing children to complete pencil-and-paper tasks all year will not make them any more prepared to successfully complete standardized tests according to their abilities. Rather, I would argue that children with lots of concrete experiences and higher level applications of the curriculum will fare better on standardized tests than will students taught traditionally.

Good test takers aren't successful because they know all the content by heart. They're good test takers because they can infer and deduce information and make correct choices a high percentage of the time. This may suffice for the needs of a multiple-choice test, but any master teacher will tell you that students really haven't mastered a skill or concept until they can apply it in a completely novel context. For example, any standardized test can ask a student to identify the major organs in the digestive system of a fetal pig, but students who are able to take that working knowledge and identify similar organs while manually dissecting the feline digestive system demonstrate that they have truly mastered the skill. Which students would you rather have working in your laboratory? Gardner's definition of intelligence resounds clearly: the ability to create products and solve problems that are of value in one's own culture. This is the essence of authentic assessment—to be able to demonstrate understanding in rich, real-world, performance-based tasks. When students can demonstrate these kinds of abilities with regard to math, science, history, language, and the arts, then we will have truly revolutionized public education. One key to making this happen is technology.

Having said all this, what kinds of assessment should we be using? Authentic assessments certainly, but do we need to provide an authentic assessment for every skill that matches every intelligence in the classroom? Thankfully, no. Just as no one lesson should attempt to cover all the intelligences, neither should one assessment. Rather, plan your assessments globally so that in the course of any unit or project students will get the opportunity to perform assessments that will stimulate all of the intelligences. This serves a twofold purpose. First, students will have the chance to demonstrate their mastery regardless of their strengths. Second, they will be exposed to all kinds of tasks so that they have the opportunity to strengthen those intelligences that are not already well developed within.

The OPP Chart

The process for developing a sound authentic assessment task is demonstrated in an Objective, Procedure, Product (OPP) chart. An OPP chart requires teachers to refer to the original objective in a lesson, examine how well the objective is taught through the procedure of the lesson, and then identify a product that demonstrates the degree of student mastery of that original objective. (The CD-ROM accompanying this book contains a blank OPP chart in the MI_Evaluation_Tools file.)

Consider the following elements of OPP for a third-grade social studies lesson.

OBJECTIVE: Given graph paper, pencil, ruler, and markers, the learner will create a map of the classroom that includes a legend with symbols for doorways, windows, counters, closets, and furniture.

PROCEDURE:

1. Examine a variety of maps and review their features (grid, legend, compass rose).

2. Create a wall-sized mock-up sketch of the classroom with student input to help encourage thinking about everything that should be included in a map of the classroom.

3. Have students work in pairs to map the classroom accurately with a legend for doorways, windows, counters, closets, and furniture.

PRODUCT: Completed classroom maps will be evaluated for neatness and accurate placement of doorways, windows, counters, closets, and furniture in the classroom.

The completed OPP chart is shown in Table 27.

Table 27

OPP Chart for a Third-Grade Social Studies Lesson

	OBJECTIVE	PROCEDURE	PRODUCT
	Create maps on graph paper with a legend of symbols for doorways, windows, counters, closets, and furniture.	Brainstorm map elements and then have students work in pairs to create original classroom maps.	Classroom maps that are evaluated for neatness and accuracy.
INTELLIGENCES	Visual Naturalist	Visual Naturalist	Logical
BLOOM	Synthesis	Synthesis	Comprehension

This is a very well-intentioned lesson. Students are asked to apply their knowledge of maps and mapping to create original maps that use a symbol system to denote major objects in the classroom. However, look at the OPP chart in Table 27. The objective stresses the use of symbols in a legend, but the product is being evaluated for neatness and accuracy. The objective emphasizes the visual and naturalist intelligences, but the product is examined for use of the logical intelligence. Also, the objective asks students to work at the synthesis level of Bloom's taxonomy, but the evaluation is at a much lower level of the taxonomy. There is not a clear match going from left to right on the OPP chart! Perhaps the objective can be reworded to stress neatness and accuracy, or perhaps the product evaluation can be modified to emphasize the symbols in the legend rather than a clean, precise classroom map. Whatever tact the teacher devising this lesson selects, the goal will be to line up the elements of the OPP so that there is agreement all the way through the chart.

Here's another example. A seventh-grade English teacher is going to teach the soliloquy form as part of his study of *The Merchant of Venice*. Table 28 shows the OPP chart for this lesson.

This is a classic lesson we all have encountered at some point in our education. It is well intended and it is surely laudable to have students study, memorize, and recite a soliloquy as part of their study of Shakespeare. Still, look at the OPP chart in Table 28. The objective starts out as a direct, succinct, measurable goal. It emphasizes the musical/rhythmic, verbal, and logical intelligences. In the procedure, students are immersed in a specific Shakespearean soliloquy in order to gain an appreciation of the form. It follows through nicely on the objective as stated. However, look at the product. Does recitation of a dozen lines from Shakespeare demonstrate an understanding of the form and content of the soliloquy? While the objective clearly calls for application and analysis, simple recitation has students functioning at the knowledge level of Bloom's taxonomy. To make this an effective lesson, this

Table 28

OPP Chart for "The Merchant of Venice Soliloquy" Lesson

	OBJECTIVE	PROCEDURE	PRODUCT
	Analyze the elements of a Shakespearean soliloquy, including rhyme, meter, and content.	Study the form and content of a soliloquy from *The Merchant of Venice* as an example.	Recite the soliloquy from *The Merchant of Venice* from memory.
INTELLIGENCES	Musical/Rhythmic Verbal Logical	Musical/Rhythmic Verbal Logical	Musical/Rhythmic Verbal Logical
BLOOM	Application and analysis	Application and analysis	Knowledge

assessment will have to be completely rewritten. Table 29 provides a revised OPP chart for the lesson.

The lesson as shown in Table 29 consistently targets the objective through the intelligences and levels of thinking the teacher targets in the final product. The OPP chart is an effective way to line up your assessment tasks so that you can accurately measure the learning that takes place in your classroom.

Table 29

Revised OPP Chart for "The Merchant of Venice Soliloquy" Lesson

	OBJECTIVE	PROCEDURE	PRODUCT
	Analyze the elements of a Shakespearean soliloquy, including rhyme, meter, and content.	Study the form and content of a soliloquy from *The Merchant of Venice* as an example.	Analyze a second Shakespearean soliloquy and contrast the two soliloquies in terms of rhyme, meter, and content.
INTELLIGENCES	Musical/Rhythmic Verbal Logical	Musical/Rhythmic Verbal Logical	Musical/Rhythmic Verbal Logical
BLOOM	Application and analysis	Application and analysis	Application and analysis

If it all comes down to assessment, then the way in which you assess authentic tasks is extremely important. In constructing authentic assessments, devise open-ended tasks that allow each student to apply the skills and concepts you have taught in novel ways.

Ask each student to create a presentation that states the colonists' grievances against the King with at least seven specific references made to actual events that occurred between 1763 and 1775. Are you evaluating your students' knowledge of how sound waves travel? Ask your students to create their own experiment that demonstrates how to lengthen and shorten sound waves so that one can tell aurally what is happening to the sound. Is it time to assess student mastery of measuring mass? Have students construct balsa wood balance scales that can weigh up to 2 pounds accurately.

The possibilities are all around you. It simply requires you to look at assessment with a different point of reference than the way we ourselves were taught.

Rubric Construction

One excellent authentic assessment tool is the rubric. Rubrics provide quantitative evaluation of student work while offering qualitative feedback. Teachers have the standards for students in place, and students can expect input that will help them understand how their work measures up against those standards—and what they can do to improve their performance. It's a win-win situation.

Here are some suggestions for constructing rubrics:

- Use student input in creating standards for the rubric.

- Create the rubric using a spreadsheet template so that it is easy to fill in, calculate, and save.

- Identify the intelligences you are using for each of the criteria on your rubric. This will help you determine if your assessment values the same intelligences your objectives intended.

- Use highly descriptive indicators for degrees of success and include numerical weights so that students can see differentiated levels of success.

- Present the rubric to students before they begin their task so that they can keep in mind the criteria for completing the task successfully.

- Have students complete the rubric on their own work in progress. Then have them share their perceptions with you before you complete the rubric on their product.

For example, let's use the following authentic task: "In a clean, easy-to-follow format, create a presentation that states the colonists' grievances against the King, making at least seven specific references to actual events that occurred between 1763 and 1775." The rubric might look like the one shown in Table 30.

With this rubric, the student can score a maximum of 15 points. The teacher has already determined that a score of 10 or higher is needed to pass the assessment, and that a score of 9 or lower will indicate that the student has not mastered an understanding of the causes of the American Revolution. Is there any doubt that after completing this assessment both the student and teacher will know to what degree the causes of the American Revolution have been mastered in the classroom? Is there any question that students who perform at the Excellent level of the rubric will do well on questions on the causes of the American Revolution that appear on any standardized test? A well-constructed rubric is a strong teaching and assessment tool.

Digital technology can play an important role in authentic assessment. So many of the productivity tools on the computer provide great formats for presentations for culminating products. Slideshows, spreadsheets with accompanying charts and graphs, and Web sites are all effective ways to show student mastery of content, some of which cannot be very easily demonstrated through hands-on means. Imagine a presentation on the Civil Rights movement created in PowerPoint, or a chart generated from a spreadsheet containing statistical data on immigration from 1820 to 1860, or an interactive periodic table of the elements on a student-created Web page where each element's properties are linked to further information. Creating your rubric in a spreadsheet will allow you to include a digital assessment of students' work to accompany their own digital products. Welcome to the Information Age!

Whether students do tasks on the computer, in hard-copy format, or as a performance, capture the results by using a digital camera or scanner so that you have a digital record of the students' artifacts to go along with the digital rubric. Where will you put all these digital artifacts? Why, in a digital portfolio, of course! Digital portfolios allow you to collect samples of authentic assessment tasks over time as well as the rubrics you use to assess them. Digital portfolios open up all kinds of possibilities for authentic assessment tasks that challenge students to solve problems and create products to demonstrate learning. You can set up individual student folders on floppy disks, a computer hard drive, a network server, or even on the Internet. With password protection for each folder, you can keep track of student work throughout the year without those bulky manila folders cluttering up several drawers of your filing cabinet. Digital portfolios are compact, easy to retrieve, and always easy to modify as you see the need.

Consider the digital portfolio taken to its full potential. Student portfolios can be housed on your school server or in a protected virtual environment like Blackboard or Yahoo Groups. Parents can be given their child's portfolio folder password so that they can view their child's progress from any Internet-connected computer 24 hours a day, 7 days a week. You can add an e-mail link, and parents will be able to touch base with you—on their schedules—whenever the need arises. This can be the beginning of your own virtual classroom!

Table 30

"American Revolution" Rubric

	UNSATISFACTORY 1	SATISFACTORY 2	EXCELLENT 3	TOTAL
Selected an effective medium to complete the task. (Visual)	Did not display grievances.	Displayed grievances.	Displayed grievances in a compelling, forceful way.	
Created presentation in a clean, easy-to-follow format. (Verbal)	Messy, hard to read or understand.	Presentation was clean, neat, and easy to follow.	Presentation was clean, easy to follow, and provided a greater understanding of the grievances.	
Included 7 or more events that occurred between 1763 and 1775. (Logical)	Presentation contained fewer than 7 events or contained fictional events.	Presentation included 7 historic events that occurred between 1763 and 1775.	Presentation included more than 7 historic events that occurred between 1763 and 1775.	
Explained how each event was a justified grievance from the colonists' point of view. (Intrapersonal)	Listed events without explaining their impact on colonists.	Explained how each event was a justified grievance from the colonists' point of view.	Explained how each event was a justified grievance and showed how each event built on previous resentments.	
Presented the final product to the class successfully. (Interpersonal)	Presented an incomplete or inaccurate presentation.	Presented a presentation that successfully explained the colonists' grievances.	Presented a presentation that successfully explained the colonists' grievances and successfully answered audience questions on the subject.	

SCALE: 13-15   Excellent mastery of the causes of the American Revolution.
10-12   Sufficient mastery of the causes of the American Revolution.
0-9   Student has not mastered the causes of the American Revolution.

Transforming the Classroom

All of the wonderful possibilities described in this chapter are still technotraditionalist in nature. We are trying to accomplish traditional tasks using digital tools—rubrics, work samples, portfolios. Eventually I foresee technoconstructivist educators who dare to transform the classroom by the very formats of the assessments they use. Imagine standardized tests wherein students participate in virtual simulations to respond to stimuli and solve problems as they appear before them within the context of real-world situations. Instead of filling in bubbles by selecting the letter that corresponds to a multiple-choice answer, students will sit at a computer and interact with a generative software application that provides the stimulus and records the students' responses: a virtual canoe trip down a state scenic river, a digital science experiment in which the student controls the process, or a cyber Shakespearean soliloquy that takes place against the backdrop of the Globe theater. The tests will still be norm-referenced and evaluated for validity and reliability, but students will have so many more opportunities to apply their knowledge and show off their learning through all the different intelligences. Technology is the vehicle upon which MI can transport education into the future.

For all the possibilities for technology and MI discussed in this book, there is no one set way to address the implications of MI in instruction. Rather, the discussion has been focused on opening the doors of education to allow for the possibilities of what can take place when these powerful movements in education are allowed to realize their potential. The intelligences will function and flourish as you offer open-ended tasks that will allow them to do so. They are not meant to be labels or categories for teachers to keep a record of. They function in your classroom at some level whether you acknowledge them or not!

As for that classroom of the future where students can demonstrate their mastery of content regardless of how their intelligences are distributed, it's not as far away as you may think. State departments of education are already moving toward statewide automated standardized testing. Once that is accomplished, test formats dictated by the limitations of pencil and paper will begin to give way to the possibilities I have discussed in this book. Dr. Gardner has asked questions that must be answered, and technology is leading the way. What an exciting time to be in education!

Reflections

1 How does assessment dictate the kinds of instructional strategies you choose?

2 Would digital student portfolios encourage you to include technology more frequently in your instruction?

3 How do you envision technoconstructivist assessment formats?

Appendix A

Multiple Intelligences Survey for Students

For each statement, enter a number one (1) if you agree with the statement or enjoy the activity being described. Enter a number zero (0) if you do not.		
Name:		**1 or 0**
EXAMPLE:	Swimming.	1
I like.....	Sorting things into groups.	
	Thinking about life.	
	Picturing things in my mind.	
	Working with my hands.	
	Studying patterns.	
	Keeping things in order.	
	Studying with a partner.	
	Seeing how everything fits in the big picture.	
	Learning a new language.	
	Being right.	
	Listening to sounds in nature.	
	Moving around.	
	Making up nonsense words.	
	Following directions.	
	Protecting nature.	
	Decorating a room.	
	Chatting online.	
	Having strong feelings about things.	
	Playing sports.	
	Studying religion.	
	Making art.	
	Moving to a beat.	
	Writing stories.	
	Solving problems.	
	Completing a wordfind puzzle.	
	Being on a team.	

MULTIPLE INTELLIGENCES SURVEY FOR STUDENTS		
I like...	Drawing maps.	
	Hiking and camping.	
	Playing an instrument.	
	Practicing sign language.	
	Studying art.	
	Having things neat and tidy.	
	Studying different countries.	
	Being fair.	
	Writing in a diary.	
	Speaking up when I see something wrong.	
	Rhyming words.	
	Watching a play.	
	Working in a garden.	
	Figuring out math problems.	
	Being a good friend.	
	Listening to music.	
	Talking on the phone.	
	Wondering about the universe.	
	Exercising.	
	Visiting national parks.	
	Feeling good about my work.	
	Remembering rhymes or words to songs.	
	Creating graphs and charts.	
	Making timelines.	
	Having a debate.	
	Getting along with others.	
	Putting together a puzzle.	
	Reading charts and tables.	
	Making arts and crafts.	
	Helping the poor.	
	Being with other people.	
	Answering riddles.	
	Watching a video.	

MULTIPLE INTELLIGENCES SURVEY FOR STUDENTS		
I like...	Writing letters.	
	Dancing.	
	Having background noise while I work.	
	Working alone.	
	Observing the stars and planets.	
	Using my imagination.	
	Knowing before something is about to happen.	
	Learning about animals.	
	Listening to all kinds of music.	
	Using tools.	
	Joining a club.	
	Discussing why the world is the way it is.	
	Being a leader.	
	Giving a speech.	
	Marching to a beat.	
	Knowing why I should do something.	
	Keeping things neat.	
	Summarizing ideas.	
	Building things.	
	Recycling waste.	
	Taking notes.	
	Working with others.	
	Planning things in my mind.	
	Wondering about life on other planets.	
	Being treated fairly.	
	Going to the zoo.	
	Making lists.	
	Playing charades.	
	Listening to a story.	
	Reading books.	
	Being around other people.	
	Spending time outdoors.	

Appendix B

Primary Grades Multiple Intelligences Survey
Circle each picture that shows an activity you like to do.

Student Name: _____

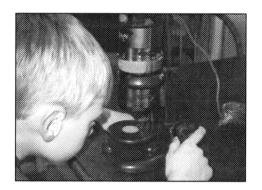

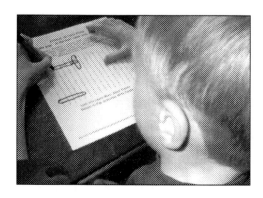

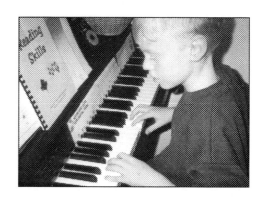

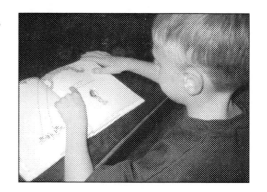

Totals:

Verbal/Linguistic	_____		Naturalist	_____
Interpersonal	_____		Bodily/Kinesthetic	_____
Logical/Mathematical	_____		Existential	_____
Intrapersonal	_____		Musical/Rhythmic	_____
Visual/Spatial	_____			

Appendix C

Bibliography

Armstrong, T. (2000). *Multiple Intelligences in the Classroom (2nd edition)*. Alexandria, Virginia: Association for Supervision and Curriculum Development.

Asen, S. (1992). *Teaching and Learning with Technology.* Alexandria, Virginia: Association for Supervision and Curriculum Development.

Bloom, B. (ed). (1956). *Taxonomy of Educational Objectives: The Classification of Educational Goals.* New York: Longman, Green.

Gardner, H. (1999). *The Disciplined Mind.* New York: Simon & Schuster.

Gardner, H. (1999). *Intelligence Reframed.* New York: Basic Books.

Gardner, H. (1991). *Multiple Intelligences: Theory into Practice.* New York: Basic Books.

Gardner, H. (1991). *The Unschooled Mind: How Children Think and How Schools Should Teach.* New York: Basic Books.

Gardner, H. (1983). *Frames of Mind.* New York: Basic Books.

Harris, J. (1998). *Virtual Architecture: Designing and Directing Curriculum-Based Telecomputing.* Eugene, Oregon: International Society for Technology in Education.

Howard, B.C. et al. (Summer, 2000). "The Experience of Constructivism: Transforming Teacher Epistemology." *Journal of Research on Computing in Education,* pp. 455-465.

Jacobs, H.H. (1997). *Mapping the Big Picture: Integrating Curriculum and Assessment K-12.* Alexandria, Virginia: Association for Supervision and Curriculum Development.

Marzano, R.J., et al. (1993) *Assessing Student Outcomes.* Alexandria, Virginia: Association for Supervision and Curriculum Development.

McKenzie, J. (1999). *How Teachers Learn Technology Best.* Bellingham, Washington: FNO Press.

McKenzie, W. (1998). *I Think…..Therefore…..M.I.!* (1998) http://surfaquarium.com/im.htm.

Mitra, A., & Steffensmeier, T. (Spring, 2000). "Changes in Student Attitudes and Student Computers in a Computer-Enriched Environment." *Journal of Research on Computing in Education,* pp. 417-433.

Moursund, D. (1999). *Project-Based Learning Using Information Technology.* Eugene, Oregon: International Society for Technology in Education.

Noon, S. (October, 1998). "4 Stages of Technology Adoption: Part One—Training the Pre-Literate End User to use Computers in the Classroom." *Classroom Connect,* p. 11.

Noon, S. (November, 1998). "4 Stages of Technology Adoption: Part Two—Training the Software Technician to use Technology in the Classroom." *Classroom Connect,* p. 11.

Noon, S. (December , 1998, January 1999). "4 Stages of Technology Adoption: Part Three—The Electronic Traditionalist." *Classroom Connect,* p. 21.

Noon, S. (February, 1999). "4 Stages of Technology Adoption: Part Four—Training Techno-Constructivists." (February, 1999). *Classroom Connect,* p. 11.

Vaille, J.A. (ed). (1998). *Guidelines for the Evaluation of Instructional Technology Resources.* Eugene, Oregon: International Society for Technology in Education.

Wheeler, M., et al. (2000). *National Educational Technology Standards for Students: Connecting Curriculum and Technology.* Eugene, Oregon: International Society for Technology in Education.

Wiggins, G., and McTighe, J. (1998). *Understanding by Design.* Alexandria, Virginia: Association for Supervision and Curriculum Development.

Appendix D

ISTE National Educational Technology Standards (NETS) and Performance Indicators for Teachers

All classroom teachers should be prepared to meet the following standards and performance indicators.

I. **TECHNOLOGY OPERATIONS AND CONCEPTS**—Teachers demonstrate a sound understanding of technology operations and concepts. *Teachers:*

    A. demonstrate introductory knowledge, skills, and understanding of concepts related to technology (as described in the ISTE National Educational Technology Standards for Students).

    B. demonstrate continual growth in technology knowledge and skills to stay abreast of current and emerging technologies.

II. **PLANNING AND DESIGNING LEARNING ENVIRONMENTS AND EXPERIENCES**—Teachers plan and design effective learning environments and experiences supported by technology. *Teachers:*

    A. design developmentally appropriate learning opportunities that apply technology-enhanced instructional strategies to support the diverse needs of learners.

    B. apply current research on teaching and learning with technology when planning learning environments and experiences.

    C. identify and locate technology resources and evaluate them for accuracy and suitability.

    D. plan for the management of technology resources within the context of learning activities.

    E. plan strategies to manage student learning in a technology-enhanced environment.

III. **TEACHING, LEARNING, AND THE CURRICULUM**—Teachers implement curriculum plans that include methods and strategies for applying technology to maximize student learning. *Teachers:*

    A. facilitate technology-enhanced experiences that address content standards and student technology standards.

    B. use technology to support learner-centered strategies that address the diverse needs of students.

    C. apply technology to develop students' higher-order skills and creativity.

    D. manage student learning activities in a technology-enhanced environment.

IV. **ASSESSMENT AND EVALUATION**—Teachers apply technology to facilitate a variety of effective assessment and evaluation strategies. *Teachers:*

    A. apply technology in assessing student learning of subject matter using a variety of assessment techniques.

    B. use technology resources to collect and analyze data, interpret results, and communicate findings to improve instructional practice and maximize student learning.

    C. apply multiple methods of evaluation to determine students' appropriate use of technology resources for learning, communication, and productivity.

V. PRODUCTIVITY AND PROFESSIONAL PRACTICE—Teachers use technology to enhance their productivity and professional practice. *Teachers:*

A. use technology resources to engage in ongoing professional development and lifelong learning.

B. continually evaluate and reflect on professional practice to make informed decisions regarding the use of technology in support of student learning.

C. apply technology to increase productivity.

D. use technology to communicate and collaborate with peers, parents, and the larger community in order to nurture student learning.

VI. SOCIAL, ETHICAL, LEGAL, AND HUMAN ISSUES—Teachers understand the social, ethical, legal, and human issues surrounding the use of technology in PK–12 schools and apply that understanding in practice. *Teachers:*

A. model and teach legal and ethical practice related to technology use.

B. apply technology resources to enable and empower learners with diverse backgrounds, characteristics, and abilities.

C. identify and use technology resources that affirm diversity.

D. promote safe and healthy use of technology resources.

E. facilitate equitable access to technology

Appendix E

ISTE National Educational Technology Standards (NETS) and Performance Indicators for Administrators

All school administrators should be prepared to meet the following standards and performance indicators. These standards are a national consensus among educational stakeholders of what best indicates effective school leadership for comprehensive and appropriate use of technology in schools.

I. LEADERSHIP AND VISION—Educational leaders inspire a shared vision for comprehensive integration of technology and foster an environment and culture conducive to the realization of that vision. *Educational leaders:*

A. facilitate the shared development by all stakeholders of a vision for technology use and widely communicate that vision.

B. maintain an inclusive and cohesive process to develop, implement, and monitor a dynamic, long-range, and systemic technology plan to achieve the vision.

C. foster and nurture a culture of responsible risk-taking and advocate policies promoting continuous innovation with technology.

D. use data in making leadership decisions.

E. advocate for research-based effective practices in use of technology.

F. advocate, on the state and national levels, for policies, programs, and funding opportunities that support implementation of the district technology plan.

II. LEARNING AND TEACHING—Educational leaders ensure that curricular design, instructional strategies, and learning environments integrate appropriate technologies to maximize learning and teaching. *Educational leaders:*

A. identify, use, evaluate, and promote appropriate technologies to enhance and support instruction and standards-based curriculum leading to high levels of student achievement.

B. facilitate and support collaborative technology-enriched learning environments conducive to innovation for improved learning.

C. provide for learner-centered environments that use technology to meet the individual and diverse needs of learners.

D. facilitate the use of technologies to support and enhance instructional methods that develop higher-level thinking, decision-making, and problem-solving skills.

E. provide for and ensure that faculty and staff take advantage of quality professional learning opportunities for improved learning and teaching with technology.

III. PRODUCTIVITY AND PROFESSIONAL PRACTICE—Educational leaders apply technology to enhance their professional practice and to increase their own productivity and that of others. *Educational leaders:*

A. model the routine, intentional, and effective use of technology.

B. employ technology for communication and collaboration among colleagues, staff, parents, students, and the larger community.

C. create and participate in learning communities that stimulate, nurture, and support faculty and staff in using technology for improved productivity.

D. engage in sustained, job-related professional learning using technology resources.

E. maintain awareness of emerging technologies and their potential uses in education.

F. use technology to advance organizational improvement.

IV. SUPPORT, MANAGEMENT, AND OPERATIONS—Educational leaders ensure the integration of technology to support productive systems for learning and administration. *Educational leaders:*

A. develop, implement, and monitor policies and guidelines to ensure compatibility of technologies.

B. implement and use integrated technology-based management and operations systems.

C. allocate financial and human resources to ensure complete and sustained implementation of the technology plan.

D. integrate strategic plans, technology plans, and other improvement plans and policies to align efforts and leverage resources.

E. implement procedures to drive continuous improvements of technology systems and to support technology replacement cycles.

V. ASSESSMENT AND EVALUATION—Educational leaders use technology to plan and implement comprehensive systems of effective assessment and evaluation. *Educational leaders:*

A. use multiple methods to assess and evaluate appropriate uses of technology resources for learning, communication, and productivity.

B. use technology to collect and analyze data, interpret results, and communicate findings to improve instructional practice and student learning.

C. assess staff knowledge, skills, and performance in using technology and use results to facilitate quality professional development and to inform personnel decisions.

D. use technology to assess, evaluate, and manage administrative and operational systems.

VI. SOCIAL, LEGAL, AND ETHICAL ISSUES—Educational leaders understand the social, legal, and ethical issues related to technology and model responsible decision-making related to these issues. *Educational leaders:*

A. ensure equity of access to technology resources that enable and empower all learners and educators.

B. identify, communicate, model, and enforce social, legal, and ethical practices to promote responsible use of technology.

C. promote and enforce privacy, security, and online safety related to the use of technology.

D. promote and enforce environmentally safe and healthy practices in the use of technology.

E. participate in the development of policies that clearly enforce copyright law and assign ownership of intellectual property developed with district resources.

This material was originally produced as a project of the Technology Standards for School Administrators Collaborative.